Calladitas RISING

RECLAIMING YOUR POWER, STRENGTH, AND VOICE

Compiled by
Gabriela Ramírez-Arellano
y Esmeralda Aharon

Calladitas Rising

Reclaiming Your Power, Strength, and Voice

Gabriela Ramírez-Arellano y Esmeralda Aharon

Published by Latinas Rising, LLC

Cover, Interior Design, and Project Management:
  Davis Creative Publishing, DavisCreativePublishing.com
Writing Coach and Editor: Jacqueline Duty

Publisher's Cataloging-in-Publication
(Provided by Cassidy Cataloguing Services, Inc.)
Names: Ramírez-Arellano, Gabriela, compiler. | Aharon, Esmeralda, compiler.
Title: Calladitas rising : reclaiming your power, strength, and voice / compiled by Gabriela Ramírez-Arellano y Esmeralda Aharon.
Description: [O'Fallon, Missouri] : Latinas Rising, LLC, [2024] | In English with some Spanish phrases.
Identifiers: ISBN: 979-8-9913987-0-1 (paperback) | 979-8-9913987-1-8 (ebook | LCCN: 2024917573
Subjects: LCSH: Hispanic American women--Biography. | Hispanic American women--Social conditions--Literary collections. | Hispanic American women--Psychology--Literary collections. | Self-esteem in women--Literary collections. | Identity (Psychology)--Literary collections. | Sex role--Literary collections. | LCGFT: Biographies. | Self-help publications. | BISAC: BIOGRAPHY & AUTOBIOGRAPHY / Hispanic & Latino. | SELF-HELP / Motivational & Inspirational. | LITERARY COLLECTIONS / American / Hispanic & Latino.
Classification:LCC: E184.S75 C35 2024 | DDC: 305.48868073--dc23

"As someone who believes in the transformative power of art, I see Calladitas Rising *empowering Latina voices. By sharing their stories, the authors are not only reclaiming their voices but also setting an example for future generations to be proud of who they are. Supporting this project is Cartel's way of ensuring that our stories—like art—continue to inspire and elevate our community."*

– CARLOS ZAMORA, Founder & Chief Creative Officer, Cartel

"We are excited to support Calladitas Rising *because we are committed to amplifying underrepresented voices in STEM. Sharing our journeys is essential to encouraging and inspiring others and showing them that they, too, can be successful and thrive in STEM."*

– Society of Hispanic Professional Engineers, St. Louis, MO

"As an author and proud supporter of Calladitas Rising, *I hope our stories inspire others to find the strength and courage to speak up and be heard."*

–TANIA SIMON-INTERIAN, Tania Interian Agency, State Farm

"I believe that having a voice is as important as being seen. Calladitas Rising *empowers people whose voices are not typically heard to be heard and whose faces are not usually seen to be seen. I hope this project inspires a generation of leaders. This is why Midwest BankCentre chose to support this effort—it's ultimately about using our platform to amplify bold leadership."*

– ORVIN KIMBROUGH, Chairman & CEO, Midwest BankCentre

*"*Calladitas Rising *is a powerful example of the strength and resilience of Latinas who refuse to be silenced and are ready to stand in their power. I am excited about supporting the authors because it reflects my commitment to uplifting and empowering the Latino community."*

– JOSE PONCE, President, Expert Partners

"*Writing my story for* Calladitas Rising *has been empowering, but working alongside these phenomenal Latinas has given me a new sense of purpose. I now see that I'm helping so many and contributing to something far bigger than myself.*"

– JOSEPHINE SANTANA, MSgt, USAF

"*We are multifaceted beings, capable of great things. Yet, when it comes to supporting other women, we sometimes fall short. As a woman of color, I've seen the transformative power of sisterhood; that's why I am supporting* Calladitas Rising. *Let's break down barriers and create a space where we can lift each other up and thrive.*"

– LEENNA CHOUDHARRY, Founder, Placement Expert USA
and #1 International Bestselling Author

"Calladitas Rising *is a remarkable anthology that gives Latina women the platform to share their powerful stories. I believe in empowering women to embrace their unique journeys, and this book is evidence of the strength that comes from turning challenges into triumphs and voices into catalysts for change.*"

– DEBI CORRIE, CEO of Acumaxum and author of *Loving Failure*

DEDICATION

To my children, Adriana, Marcela, and Edward—
you are my inspiration, my strength, and the reason
I strive to make the world a better place.
Though Marcela and Edward are no longer with us,
their memory continues to guide me,
and this anthology is dedicated to them and to all
who find the courage to use their voices to create lasting change.

–GABRIELA RAMÍREZ-ARELLANO

To my beloved children, Avi, Ari, Hillel, and Yair:
You inspire me every day to live with courage, resilience, and
purpose, reminding me to never give up in adversity.
Though Hillel is no longer with us, his memory
fuels my devotion to God and country,
granting me the stamina to act justly, love mercy,
and walk humbly, while empowering others to
find their own power, strength, and voice.

–ESMERALDA AHARON

TRIGGER WARNING:
Several chapters in this book describe the authors'
experiences overcoming the effects of violence—
including childhood sexual assault and marital abuse,
self-harm and suicide—as well as less-than-positive
coping strategies for the resulting trauma, such as
sexual acting out and overuse of alcohol and both
prescribed and illegal street drugs.

TABLE OF CONTENTS

Foreword

My journey as a Latina has familiar threads. I was born in Mexico. I lived in Europe for many years, working most of those years for the United Nations. There, my career was as a diplomat, a social activist, and a social marketer of global humanitarian campaigns. Ten years ago, when I moved to the United States, I soon discovered I belonged to the Hispanic community. I had no idea what this meant.

I always begin understanding something new by examining facts and data. What I learned was that Latinos are enormous contributors to the economy and culture. Latinos remain true believers of the American Dream—that hard work and education pave the path to success. But I found a huge gap between the perception of Latinos and the reality.

Stereotypes, prejudice, and other biases shaped our narrative, not the facts. Within our own ranks, we are so diverse that our community is fragmented and divided. But we all shared one thing—we believe in progress. Uniting us as a community and raising awareness of our contributions within the community and beyond became the driving principles behind my founding the We Are All Human Foundation and its Hispanic Star initiative six years ago.

Changing perceptions is difficult work. What became clear to us quickly is that we *must* own our narrative. That is not only how we correct the image of us publicly, but also how we gain the strength, the confidence, and the determination to lead our individual lives. But for so long, the Hispanic community has lived with the absence of role models. Without them, it has been hard to counter the stereotypes or break down the barriers because the old adage is true—you have to see it to be it.

This is particularly true for Latinas. Here are some facts about us: We lead the charge in our community for higher education degrees. In the past 20 years, Latinas have led the charge in getting Bachelor of Arts degrees, jumping from 1 million women in 2001 to 3.5 million three years ago. Yet we are paid less than half of what a white man earns, less than any other ethnic group. And our representation in the senior ranks of the corporate world is less than 5%.

Latinas are huge entrepreneurs, outpacing white male and female entrepreneurs in revenue growth, employees, and payroll. And yet, we have limited access to capital—the lowest rate of business loans from local and national banks.

The very values that have served us so well are often distorted, misinterpreted, and devalued. Our love of family is seen as a lack of commitment when it should indicate our commitment to the team, our ability to keep many balls up in the air at once, and a spirit of collaboration. Accents are perceived as a lack of understanding English rather than a sign that we speak multiple languages. One of the first studies we undertook as a foundation asked people to characterize Latinas— every descriptor was about physical looks. No wonder too often we have remained silent.

Telling our own stories is the strongest way to pierce the bubble of misinformation. It is also the surest path to building our own networks, forging our own power base, and helping countless Latinas learn from our stories, strategies, and successes.

Gabriela Ramírez-Arellano understands both the power and the process of building a Latina business community. As an entrepreneur, a business consultant, and a business advocate, she has come to find her greatest joy in helping Hispanic entrepreneurs understand and find the resources they need to succeed. Making connections is instinctive and something she uses to help the Hispanic community in St. Louis, Missouri. She also understands the importance of our voices—they connect us, they empower us, and they help us unlock our potential.

In creating *Calladitas Rising*, Gabriela and her co-founder of this project, Esmeralda Aharon, give voice to many Latinas. Esmeralda is a builder of belonging, dedicated to fostering Diversity, Equity, and Inclusion (DEI) at Saint Louis University School of Medicine. Her background spans a 26-year Air Force career writing policy and regulations. As a bilingual speaker, Esmeralda bridges connections through her military service to the civilian and veteran communities. She is committed to uniting individuals and driving positive change with passion and dedication.

Together, Esmeralda and Gabriela not only amplify the voices of Latinas but also reveal the intersectionality of their experiences. The women in this anthology have much to share in their own life stories. They share their journeys, hardships, adversity, and barriers. But we also share the moments of inspiration, realization, and transformation. It is easy to find ourselves throughout these pages. It is also possible to find new hope, new ideas, and new confidence in them.

This was no doubt an enormous undertaking, but Esmeralda and Gabriela have deftly painted a portrait of Latinas on the rise, using our strength and resilience, our love of family, our hard work, entrepreneurial instincts, persistence, and indomitable spirit to build better lives, unlock our potential. *Calladitas Rising* is a labor of love and one worthy of your attention. I know you will find the voices compelling and inspiring. You might even find yourself changed by it.

–Claudia Romo Edelman

Founder and CEO, We Are All Human Foundation,

and A La Latina Podcast

Claudia Romo Edelman is a global mobilization expert, catalyst for social change, and marketer for social causes. She is a recognized speaker, activist, thought leader and author, and upcoming entrepreneur. Claudia is the founder of the We Are All Human Foundation and co-host of the podcast "A la Latina: The Playbook to Succeed Being Your Authentic Self." She is also currently starting a family business. She is a Mexican-Swiss diplomat with more than 25 years of experience leading marketing and advocacy for global organizations, including the World Economic Forum, UNICEF, the Global Fund to Fight AIDS, Tuberculosis and Malaria, and the United Nations. She speaks six languages, has two children, and enjoys sports and traveling.

Gabriela Ramírez-Arellano

My Voice, Mi Poder:
Finding My Voice and Power

Finding my voice was hard work. It took so long to even realize I had something to say.

It was a journey filled with obstacles, self-doubt, and social pressures that seemed to constantly remind me that I had to shrink, to fit into the expectations others had for me. It's a journey that begins in silence and moments of introspection and culminates in finally *enough* and the decision to step into my power, to stop fitting into others' expectations.

Growing up, I often felt the weight of expectations on me. As a first-generation Latina, I still carry the pressure of being the oldest and the cultural narratives that emphasize humility and keeping the peace, usually by not speaking up. Growing up, I was taught that being respectful meant following the crowd, following the rules, and paying attention to what others said about me—*el que diran*. Rarely was I encouraged to speak up for myself, to assert myself, or to speak up for what I believed in, what was right.

I was a good student, an obedient daughter, and rarely had any friends. I stayed out of trouble, and I believed that by conforming to these roles, I was good. Deep inside, there was a longing, a restlessness that I couldn't quite express—my voice remained muted.

Being at the University of Missouri was a transformative time for me. Surrounded by so many different people and exposed to new ways of thinking, I started to question the limitations I had placed on myself and those that had been placed on me. I realized for the first time that I had opinions that were different from my family's, and I began to realize that I had things to say; and sometimes, saying them out loud made me—not a good daughter.

Although I was an introvert, I did start to understand that my perspective was valuable, that my experiences and insights mattered. This realization was both liberating and scary at the same time.

The true test of my newfound voice came much later, during a difficult marriage. I found myself once again shrinking, this time within the confines of a relationship that stifled my spirit. I was so busy surviving in the marriage that I started to see the bad example I was setting for my daughters. I was stuck in a relationship that felt like I had no other choice, and yet I could see there was another way. The weight of expectations, both cultural and personal, weighed heavy on me, and I stayed far too long.

The breaking point came the day Adriana, my oldest, asked me why I was still in the marriage. She was asking me why I chose to be there. All this time I had tried to hide the difficulties, telling myself *this* was normal. *This* was all I could aspire to. Again, muting the voices and the reality of my situation.

That night, we left our home with only the clothes on our backs and a spare set of clothes I had thought to hide in the car. It was the start of a tough and crazy time, but in the middle of all the chaos, there was a moment of complete clarity. Through my daughter's eyes, I could no longer lie to myself. I could no longer unsee the reality of what had become my life.

The divorce was not just an end; it was a beginning, a catalyst for change and self-discovery. I thought of it as a reinvention because that's what I had to do, reinvent myself. In the aftermath of my divorce, I found myself in the public assistance office in Michigan, applying for cash assistance, food, and work. I spent months living on my sister's couch, trying to put these new pieces together. That spring, there were a lot of firsts as I applied for my first job, figured out how to make a living wage, and figured out where we were going to live.

In finding that first job, I found my true superpower: helping others and speaking Spanish. My heritage, which I had once taken for granted, became my greatest asset. It hit me that my ability to switch between different cultures and languages was a secret weapon I had hidden, even from myself, while I was trying to fit into the life I had been living. These superpowers were a bridge that connected me to other people and made what I did matter even more.

As I found my voice, I became passionate about helping others find theirs. I understood the struggles, the fears, and the social pressures that silence so many of us. This empathy fueled my desire to create spaces where the voices of the silenced could be heard, respected, and amplified. Small business development found me, and the work allowed me to support Spanish-speaking business owners and aspiring business owners in Southwest Detroit.

Speaking became a vital part of this mission, and Spanish was a catalyst. It allowed me to connect with a broader community, to reach those who were often marginalized and unheard. It was a reminder that our voices, in any language, have power. By embracing my voice, heritage, and language, I helped others find their voices and stand tall in their own journeys. By owning my language and background, I've helped others find their own voices and be proud of who they are.

In 2016, my reinvention continued, and I moved to St. Louis. I co-launched the Auténtico Podcast with the mission of using it as a megaphone to uplift, empower, and give a voice to Latinos. The podcast became a platform for sharing stories of resilience, success, and advocacy within our community. Through Auténtico, we highlighted the achievements of Latinx leaders, discussed pressing issues, and provided a space for open dialogue and mutual support. When St. Louis Public Radio picked up the podcast as part of the *We Live Here* series, it was a dream come true, and that experience reinforced my belief in the power of storytelling and the importance of representation.

Finding my voice has not just been about personal empowerment; it's also been about advocacy. It's about using my voice to speak truth to power, to challenge injustices, and to advocate for the things I am passionate about. This means standing up for minority business owners and language access and against anti-immigrant sentiments and political rhetoric, particularly in Missouri, where these issues are often divisive and contentious.

Advocacy isn't just about speaking out. It's about standing strong in the face of doubt, hate, and even fear. It's about risking everything for something you believe in, knowing it will change lives. That's the spark that drove the work that Lourdes Treviño Bailon and I did when we created STLJuntos during the darkest days of the pandemic. We fought for our community, demanding access to basic needs like language services, healthcare, and food. But our work is far from over.

One of the key lessons I've learned during the last 10 years is the importance of community. Finding my voice has not happened in isolation. It's something I have been able to grow into with the support and encouragement of others. These experiences have taught me the power of collaboration and empowering each other. It is important to surround ourselves with people who uplift us, challenge us, *and* hold us accountable. These relationships are crucial in helping us stay true to our values, navigate challenges, and amplify our voices. I was able to lean into collaboration, starting with the first anthology that I participated in. Fulfilling a dream of being an author and getting outside my comfort zone opened doors of possibility for me because someone opened that first door for me.

At the heart of finding my voice has been the journey of being authentic. It took a long time for me to embrace who I am, with all my strengths, weaknesses, and unique experiences. I work hard to reject the pressures to conform and instead celebrate my individuality. When I speak from a place of authenticity, my voice resonates more deeply and has a more lasting impact.

There are still days when the naysayers' expectations quiet me and lead to doubt. When their "Who do you think you are?" makes me question if I can lead. And so, the journey continues. Finding my voice has been a transformative journey that has required courage, resilience, and a commitment to being uncomfortable. It has required me to break free from the constraints of social expectations and empower myself and others to speak up. It made me realize I need to break free from what society expects of me—that I have the strength to stand up for myself, to encourage others to do the same, and to advocate for what I believe in.

As women, particularly as Latinas, we have the potential to make waves that will change the world—the power to create a ripple effect of change. By discovering our unique voices and utilizing them with confidence, we can ignite a fire that inspires others, ignites positive change, and dismantles injustices that continue to hold us back. Let's make a pact to support and uplift each other, always striving to create an environment where growth, empowerment, and collaboration thrive. In doing so, we not only transform our own lives but also pave the way for future generations of women to rise, speak out, and make their mark on the world.

Imagine a world where our voices can be heard loud and clear, where our stories are listened to, and our dreams are celebrated. We can make that happen!

If you are reading this, consider this *your* call to action! The world is waiting for your brilliance, your passion, and your unwavering determination to make a mark. I invite you to keep inspiring each other. Continue to make your presence known. It's time to show the world what you're made of!

Gabriela's journey from Mexico to the United States has been deeply influenced by her immigrant experience. Her commitment to making a difference isn't just a choice; it's an intrinsic part of her being, a way of paying forward the support she and her family received, and a way of championing causes that are greater than herself.

Returning to St. Louis in 2016, Gabriela embarked on a mission to uplift small businesses, foster economic growth, and ensure language access was available. Her work at CORTEX and the BALSA Foundation reflects her dedication to empowering entrepreneurs in underserved communities and building strong local business relationships. Her impact has been recognized with honors as an Influential Business Woman and Woman of Achievement.

Gabriela's passion for elevating bilingual Latinx voices led to the creation of the Auténtico Podcast and We Live Here Auténtico, platforms that amplify stories and inspire others.

Through her work, including co-founding STLJuntos during the pandemic, Gabriela honors her children, Adriana, Marcela, and Edward, who drive her work to create a better world.

Contact information for Gabriela can be accessed here.

Esmeralda Aharon

Hasta La Raíz

The day my son passed away was the hardest day of my life. Born six weeks earlier on a cool October morning, he had been in my arms just hours prior. I was asleep when my husband woke me with the devastating news that our baby was no longer alive. I rushed to my lifeless baby and held him until the paramedics arrived and tried and failed to revive him. From the deepest part of my soul, I let out a loud cry of despair. This was the day I felt the most powerless, weak, and voiceless I have ever felt.

How? Why? Questions flooded my mind, but there were no answers. The hospital classified his death as sudden infant death syndrome. The days that followed are still a blur but something within me changed down to my very core. I walked to and fro, and nothing anyone did or said could bring me back my joy. That day I felt something die inside of me, *hasta la raíz*.

This life-changing moment altered my life's trajectory. My heart was overwhelmed with sorrow. While the paramedics performed CPR, I remained calm but prayed fervently, begging to God to save my son. "Please, do not take him," I implored. Despite my efforts, my son did not return. I could not understand why a loving God would take my baby. How could his passing be for good?

Raised with the belief that "all things work together for good to those who love God" (Romans 8:28), I struggled to see how this tragedy could serve a purpose. The despair was relentless. *Mi hermoso bebe* was gone. On the day of his burial, I wanted to be buried with him. The thought of joining him in death seemed the only escape from my pain.

One day while hiking, I saw some railroad tracks and considered walking straight onto them. Right then, I realized that I needed help as suicide seemed like the only solution. Later, I felt guilty for having those thoughts and I yearned for strength; it was then that the idea of joining the military came to me. This choice defied the patriarchal norms *de mi cultura* and marked me as the first person to courageously challenge and redefine cultural expectations *en mi familia*. I believed that by serving others, my heart would begin to heal. Within six months, I was on my way to Basic Military Training, determined to rebuild my life and legacy.

At 22, I left my family behind and headed to San Antonio, Texas. Little did I know the plans God had in store for me (Jeremiah 29:11). As training intensified at basic, I listened and heard women crying at night, and I felt compelled to reach out. Many accepted my offer to pray, and in praying for them, I began to heal. My heart began to soften, and I found strength through prayer and service. I was still angry at God, after all, he had taken my son, but my voice was now crying out to the Lord, and my prayers were helping me deal with my mental and spiritual state. Volunteering at the base chapel further helped dismantle the walls around my heart. I poured out my "heart like water in the presence of the Lord" (Lamentations 2:19), and gradually my spiritual health began to increase. When I cried over my son, I no longer sobbed with despair. By the end of basic training, I was closer to reclaiming my power, strength, and voice and was chosen to work in Religious Affairs, helping Airmen and their families become more spiritually fit.

Losing my son made me feel powerless, but eventually, it made me powerful. It cemented my faith and allowed me to help others find their strength. The God I had been angry with had softened my heart again. I discovered resilience and used my voice to support women in need, continuing this advocacy for 26 years through the United States Air Force (USAF) Chaplain Corps.

At the time, I had no idea that joining the military and refueling my faith would be exactly what I needed. The decision to enlist in the USAF felt like a gentle push from the Holy Spirit guiding me along the way. My faith, deeply rooted in my heritage, has been a constant source of power, encouraging me to persevere. Like the vibrant colors of red, orange, pink, and yellow gracing the cover of this book, my heritage is woven with the resilience and courage of my ancestors, filled with traditions, culture, language, and spirit. Although, as Latinas, we often face cultural norms that stifle our voices.

From a young age, I was told, "*callate mijita; calladita te ves más bonita*"—silence my daughter; you look prettier when you're quiet. This message shaped my upbringing and the lives of influential women in my family. This cultural expectation stifled not just their voices but just about any other *mujercita en la familia*. It has been the voice that rears through the back of my head while sitting "at the table" and wondering whether to speak up during a meeting. This pervasive norm tells us to remain silent even though our perspective is needed in society, and it is what inspired Gabriela and me to reach out to those amazing women to share their own stories in *Calladitas Rising*.

Despite these constant reminders to stay silent—whether through reprimands or the internalized pressure of cultural expectations—I have always felt a burning need to speak out. As a child, my faith became a guiding force, pushing me to advocate for justice and against the inequities I saw. Even when I wasn't always heard, I sensed my voice mattered, and I felt determined to use it to empower myself and those around me.

During a deployment, I witnessed the power of my voice when I addressed the living conditions at Al Udeid Air Base, just two weeks after the devastating events of 9/11 that shook America to its core. The base was austere, and everyone was living in a warehouse. Upon arrival, I saw that the living conditions were far from adequate, and I felt compelled to raise my concerns with the chaplain, who elevated them to base leadership. These concerns led to improvements, proving that speaking up can bring about meaningful change. That night, a pallet barrier was set up at the back of the warehouse to provide more privacy, and women were given the option to move into that area. This experience was a turning point for me, showing that my voice could bring about significant changes for servicewomen and the military operations. Despite the grim environment, I wasn't fazed by it, as I had faced similar conditions growing up as a young migrant farmworker.

As a child, we traveled to work the fields in Michigan, *en la labor,* alongside mis *abuelitos* and extended family, where we picked strawberries and cherries. With its extensive fruit farms, Michigan relied heavily on migrant labor, much of it provided by my people—Mexican Americans and some Mexican immigrants. According to the U.S. Department of Labor's National Agricultural Workers Survey, which began in 1989, 54% of farmworkers in the United States were of Mexican descent.

After each harvest season, my grandparents would use their earnings to buy vehicles, which they then sold in our hometown. Their entrepreneurial spirit, along with my grandmother's unwavering faith and resilience in the face of hardships, left a deep impression on me. *Abuelita* dealt with the cultural norms that expected her to be *calladita,* which she did until her passing.

Soy quien soy hasta la raíz because of the resilience, grit, and determination that my *abuelita* instilled in me. The next time you eat a strawberry or cherry, think of my *abuelita,* of me, and the countless *Chicanas* who harvested your fruits and vegetables then—and those still doing so today.

This grit reminds me of the invisible scars that I carry, evidence of the challenges I have faced and survived. Despite the internalized pressure and external factors to remain *calladita,* the Holy Spirit has been my source of strength, guiding me through moments of loss and doubt and empowering me to advocate for others. I am called to "speak up for those who cannot speak for themselves, for the rights of all who are destitute" (Proverbs 31:8), and that is why I do what I do.

Serving in the military gave me countless opportunities to support those in need. I used my position, listening skills, and voice to provide for the spiritual and religious needs of our service members and their families. It gave me great joy to witness the transformative power of faith in people's lives, knowing that neglecting this pillar from our lives can have detrimental effects. Faith has been my saving grace, and there are records of POWs surviving concentration camps and unimaginable sufferings because they practiced their faith in captivity.

Sadly, we have also seen how the absence of spirituality can take a toll. In 2019, 137 uniformed airmen and Air Force civilian employees died by suicide. From my first base, which saw 14 suicides in one year, to the end of my career, suicide has been a devastating force within our military communities.

To decrease this statistic, provide uninterrupted services during evenings and weekends, and to improve accessibility during the day, I designed the template for the *We Care Resource Guide* available in Air Mobility Command. With the support of various agencies, we launched this guide to provide essential mental, social, physical, and spiritual health resources. We titled it *We Care* to make sure people across the command knew we cared for them 24/7, 365 days a year. Although I am no longer on active duty, the work I designed continues to benefit our members and their families, strengthening their resilience—not just for the mission, but for life.

Now, as a Diversity, Equity, and Inclusion Partitioner, I advocate for healthcare equity and listen to the struggles of those from low socio-economic status like the younger me, who once picked strawberries and cherries. As a retired veteran, I champion the needs of women veterans, understanding firsthand the challenges we face when transitioning out of the military and seeking medical care, employment, etc. As a Latina and mother, I stand with people of color, having witnessed—and my children having experienced—microaggressions, even in so-called "welcoming" communities of higher learning. My faith, which calls me to care for "the least of these" (Matthew 25:40), drives me to support people with disabilities, neurodivergent individuals, the LGBTQ+ community, widows, and anyone else society has marginalized. Through Latinas Rising, I work to amplify the unique challenges faced by Latinas, offering them a platform to tell their stories starting with this anthology, as they have been *calladitas* for far too long. While this calling may have been kickstarted after the loss of my son, I believe that it was ingrained *hasta la raíz* by the Holy Spirit when I gave my life to Christ.

My calling to speak up for the plight of others is deeply rooted in faith, heritage, and a connection to *mis raíces*. Listening and advocating to those in need are the guiding principles that have helped me reclaim my power, strength, and voice. Does this mean I have stopped mourning the ones I have lost? Absolutely not. Grief is not linear, and missing the ones we love is only natural. Yet, immersing in something greater than us can aid in healing. A spiritual practice provides the courage to stand up for our values, beliefs, and justice. Proverbs 31:8 urges us to defend the voiceless, showing how faith and activism are profoundly intertwined.

Desde mis raíces, I stand strong, embrace my past, live fully in the present, and look forward with hope. My voice, shaped by the Holy Spirit and the loss of my son, and enriched by my heritage, grounds me to authentically acknowledge who I was and who I am now. Empowered by my military and advocacy experiences, it has become both my tool for change and my source of joy. *Entonces, ¡calladita jamás!*

Esmeralda Aharon is the embodiment of resilience, faith, and purpose. A first-generation American born near the U.S.-Mexico border, she overcame poverty by working as a migrant farmworker. Her journey took a transformative turn when she joined the United States Air Force, where she served for 26 years in Religious Affairs, spending over 20 months in the Middle East across four deployments and supporting service members and their families to develop spiritual resilience. After retiring from the Air Force, she became a champion for Diversity, Equity, and Inclusion at Saint Louis University School of Medicine where she promotes social and healthcare equity and directs retention programs for faculty and staff.

In 2023, she became a contributing author in the #1 international best-seller *Tenacity: The Deconstructing G.R.I.T. Collection,* and 10 months later, she is amplifying the voices of Latinas through the authorship arm of Latinas Rising LLC.

Aharon's commitment to service is unmatched, earning her The President's Volunteer Service Award, twice. Her advocacy extends to marginalized communities through The Mission Continues, STLJuntos, and as part of the Board of Directors of the Hispanic Leaders Group of Greater St. Louis. Additionally, she empowers women veterans as a founding member of Sisters in Service-Greater St. Louis.

Her accolades include the Hispanic Lifetime Achievement (Hispanic Chamber of Commerce), the LATINA Style Distinguished Military Service, 375th Air Mobility Wing Senior Noncommissioned Officer of the Year, United Service Organizations of Missouri Armed Forces Salute, and the Spirit of the Four Chaplains, among others.

A distinguished community leader, her unwavering spirit shines through her many roles: combat veteran, author, entrepreneur, mentor, yogini, and mother of four. As a lifelong learner, she is currently pursuing a doctoral degree in higher education.

Contact information for Esmeralda can be accessed here.

Susan Dealis Gobbo

From Personal Challenges to Community Impact

My journey from Brazil to the United States with my family was more than just a physical relocation; it was a transformative passage into a new life. As I stood at the gateway of this unfamiliar land, a wave of uncertainty mingled with the excitement of new beginnings. Little did I know that St. Louis, thousands of miles from my homeland, would find my voice and champion the cause of countless quiet women like me, navigating the challenges of expatriate life.

I have a bachelor's degree in physical therapy and a postgraduate degree in respiratory therapy and exercise physiology. For over 15 years, I worked at a well-known ICU department in Brazil, teaching new physical therapists and contributing to two scientific volumes. When my husband was offered an expatriate temporary position in the United States, I regarded it as an opportunity for him to achieve a career milestone and for me to have a "sabbatical." This migration also allowed my daughter and me to learn a new language, explore a strange country, and become more active in her life.

The initial years in Connecticut were thrilling yet demanding, with new experiences and obstacles owing to limited communication.

Learning a new language takes time, but life moves on. We moved to St. Louis in 2008 due to my husband's job transfer again. I had to learn about my surroundings while assisting my family with their relocation and supporting my kid at school.

Relocating feels like beginning with a blank sheet of paper, bringing emotional and mental challenges that often go unnoticed. Over time, I missed my home country, family, friends, work, routine, financial independence, and the accolades I had received there. A profession is more than a job; it shapes our identity and self-esteem. Not being allowed to continue my career in the United States seemed like losing a piece of myself, as if all my professional accomplishments had been erased. I frequently wondered, "Who am I?" This loss harmed my confidence and self-esteem, making it tough to recover.

Having to "name my new identity" when I was in a doctor's office and struggled to fill out the paperwork—especially when answering questions like "What is your profession?" and "Where do you work, your position?"—were difficult questions for me. My husband's proposal of "housewife" seemed like an ongoing internal battle. I commend and love those ladies who embrace the lifestyle of being a stay-at-home spouse. It is to be admired and celebrated; nevertheless, it is not who I am. I felt in my heart that I was meant to follow a different road. We shape our identities throughout time through our education, career, and experiences. Everything was gone, even my name. I became known as "Mauricio's wife" or "Laura's mom." I felt insignificant and uninteresting, and my ideas were dismissed.

Another issue was losing confidence; it felt as if my professional history had evaporated. My experiences were no longer relevant. Misconceptions about my education and ability due to language issues exacerbated my frustration.

Because my visa would not enable me to work, and I lacked the necessary credentials to practice as a physical therapist, I felt worthless and lost. I tried everything to find something meaningful. To fill the void, I attended multiple language courses and began volunteering. I joined the board of the Brazilian nonprofit organization and established the Portuguese Language Program. I became a Portuguese instructor, a program coordinator, in charge of hiring new instructors and developing the curriculum. This program was incorporated into the community college curricula. I became a qualified teacher of Portuguese as a heritage language. I began teaching Portuguese to companies' personnel conducting business in Brazil.

Through my English courses, I discovered that other expats experienced similar challenges. It took time for me to realize I was suffering from culture shock. This led me to research and write about it. Studies show that up to 40 percent of foreign assignments fail because spouses struggle to adjust; thus, companies should offer suitable preparation and ongoing support for expat employees and their families.

Motivated by my research and experiences, I developed a desire to help other women in similar situations understand the transition process and create a supportive community. It wasn't just a discovery; it was finding my passion and calling!

To make it happen and establish relationships with diverse communities, I had to leave my comfort zone and attend networking events. It was difficult to introduce myself amidst my insecurity and identity conflict. Despite setbacks, my desire to serve others remained strong.

My "aha" moment occurred at an event from an organization that supports immigrants. I met their executive director and several incredible people who recognized my enthusiasm for the subject, gave me credibility, and opened new opportunities. Connecting with individuals who care about us and want to see our success is priceless.

I put my research paper into action by developing a support structure for expat spouses. In 2016, the International Spouses/Expat Women Group was established. My mission was to create a haven where women struggling with expatriation difficulties could find comfort, support, and camaraderie. Women of all nationalities share stories and feel heard, accepted, and safe. It was about bonding. Today, our organization has over 900 members from over 95 countries.

I was progressively invited to join meetings and organizations in a variety of positions, including membership, committees, boards, and webinars representing international women. The more I interacted with the foreign and local communities, the more motivated I became to continue.

In 2017, we co-founded the International Mentoring Program to bring foreign women and their families together with local women in the St. Louis region to exchange experiences and learn. By welcoming internationals, both groups increase their knowledge and understanding of diverse cultures. This creates a sense of community. We have worked with over 600 women, both foreign and local. Passionate about our work, we decided to turn our program into a nonprofit organization to support more people. We have a board, advisory board, and staff. I wear many hats in this organization, including my role as Co-Founder and Program Director.

In 2022, alongside three other professional foreign-born women, I co-founded a nonprofit organization named Immigrant Professional Women Network with the mission to educate and empower immigrant professional women in St. Louis. I have contributed to American resources and motivational publications, particularly for individuals born abroad, and I am an active member of various organizations' boards and committees, promoting diversity, equity, and inclusivity.

My experiences as an expat spouse in the United States have driven me to participate in these endeavors. I am honored that my diligent efforts with the international community have been recognized. I've received various accolades along the way, fueling my passion to continue supporting the international community in the St. Louis region.

With all the projects I've launched, I've assisted wonderful, highly skilled foreign women who have fond memories of their prior lives but feel small, unproductive, and frequently depressed. I feel sad and upset for them. I want them to understand they are brave for leaving assurance and living in uncertainty, addressing challenges daily in a new language and culture. We foreigners may lack credentials and employment visas, but we must find something to satisfy our souls. I help them find suitable jobs or volunteer opportunities—the most efficient approach to filling this need, acquiring new skills, meeting new people, and gaining insight into a professional context.

It's critical to reveal our origins and accomplishments in our "previous lives." Telling our stories and upholding our customs and traditions helps us feel grounded. Learning the local language and immersing ourselves in the culture is critical for socializing and communicating. We must get outside of our comfort zones, try new things, and not be scared to make mistakes since we learn a lot from them.

Adaptation is a nonlinear process in which individuals react differently to change. Some people adjust to a strange situation in a matter of months, while others need years. It's critical to understand that changes don't have to be negative. They require time to be accepted, adapted, and rearranged. It is vital to be patient with ourselves and allow us to feel the emotions associated with this transition.

Whenever we leave our native country, we leave behind a support network of family and friends. When necessary, we must ask for friends' and family's support and seek professional mental health assistance. Connecting with other women in similar situations has been a breakthrough moment for many of our group members.

I feel proud of overcoming hurdles and barriers while relocating to the United States, learning from my experiences, and assisting other women in similar situations. I emphasize the necessity for cultural adaptability and the value of a supporting network. Through my work, I've helped many women find their identities, navigate new professional pathways, and build meaningful relationships, resulting in new friendships and a sense of belonging in this place we all now call home.

Discover the voice within you that urges for action! This is the beginning of something magnificent and expansive, capable of reaching those whose voices are suppressed. Remember, we are stronger than we frequently believe. Never be afraid to experiment. Persistence and multiple attempts, including failures, are required to achieve mastery. Embrace your potential, take bold steps, and watch as your journey unfolds into something extraordinary, touching and empowering lives along the way.

Nurtured with my parents' values, deeply embedded in my heart are core values of respect, integrity, honesty, humility, and love for my family. I could not close this chapter without acknowledging my husband, Mauricio, who has been a cornerstone of my journey, empowering me to devote myself to community work. I'm grateful to my dear husband and daughter, Laura, for giving me wings and the courage to achieve new heights. Their contributions to my life are immeasurable, and my accomplishments are a monument to their undying love and faith in me.

Susan Dealis Gobbo's journey from Brazil to the United States marked a transformative entry into a new chapter of her life. She navigated and overcame multiple challenges, learned from her setbacks, rediscovered her identity, and rebuilt herself. Transitioning from a successful healthcare professional to an impactful social entrepreneur in a new land, Susan found her calling! Through her civic work, she's supported many international women to feel heard, recover their identities, find their path, build meaningful relationships, and integrate into their new community while championing diversity, equity, and inclusiveness. Susan appreciates her husband, daughter, and friends› encouragement throughout her pathway and embraces her Latina heritage with pride and affection. Her numerous accolades for her achievements fuel her ongoing commitment to advocating for the international community. By sharing her story with vulnerability, Susan intends to resonate with and uplift other international women who may feel alone in a new country.

Contact information for Susan can be accessed here.

Jaclyn Noroño-Rodriguez

Lesson: Giving Up Is Always an Option

Caught your attention, didn't it?

It is true, though. Giving up is always an option, and it's easier in the absence of goals. Setting goals is like entering an address on the GPS. It routes you where you want to go, gives you an initial path, and reroutes you as needed. I can't pinpoint the moment I started setting goals. It was a habit my parents bestowed upon my brother and me, whether we wanted it or not. Now, I see it as a gift.

To give you a sense of how far back into my childhood goal-setting began, my notebook has Tweety Bird on the front of it. The Tweety bird on the cover of my journal reminds me of sitting after New Year's Eve dinners as a child, reviewing my goals for the year. My family and I would talk about what we achieved, what we didn't, and what we could do better the following year. While we didn't do this routine every year, it made an impression on me.

I would love to share the wisdom of a single pivotal "aha moment" I had that sparked my decision to move into a leadership role. But I don't think I consciously stepped into anything. Like everyone else, I moved through life. What made the difference was how I managed each of those challenges. The more I thought about it, the more "moments" I found met the criteria of being "pivotal." It wasn't one moment. It was a collection of them. This chapter explores five moments from my collection, the choices I faced, and the goal I was chasing.

1. When I came to the United States from Venezuela at 16...

I graduated high school at 15 years old. It was not fun to be the youngest throughout school. If you met me today, you would never guess that I was one of the quiet ones at school. I did not have a lot of friends before I immigrated. Once I started college, I quickly realized I needed to come out of my shell to survive in the United States.

I was scared of speaking because it was not in my nature to be outspoken. On top of that, I was afraid people would not understand my English since it is my second language. I had to choose between learning to be outgoing or facing the world alone. My goal was to succeed at college and make a lot of friends. So, I decided to be outgoing! I found ways to connect with people (by asking about them), plus I joined college associations to meet people, and it made all the difference!

With a few more challenges along the way, I was blessed to graduate college and start my professional career. After college, I got married and it did not go the way I thought it would.

2. When my marriage was over...

My first husband and I were married for five years. Without going into details, it did not work. I was hurt to know that the person I gave my 100 percent to, the one I thought I would spend the rest of my life with, chose to be with someone else.

My choices were to give up on love, retreat to my familiar life in Venezuela, *or* push through the pain, rise above the ashes of my marriage, and just keep going. My goals were to have a happy marriage and grow my family. And here is when reality hit: the timing of those goals is not in my control. I had done everything I could to salvage our relationship, so the only step left to take was to focus on my other goals and rise above. I started nurturing every other goal I could control. God was a big part of getting me through this time by helping me understand that I am not meant to understand.

Meanwhile, I kept growing in my professional realm. I progressed from associate to representative, to specialist, to senior specialist, to manager, and then finally to director level in sales. After my first year in the role, performance review time came.

3. When I failed at work...

I had worked so hard, yet barely achieved half of my sales target. I felt awful. I am a goal-driven person! Not meeting my goal physically hurt. When my boss, the CEO, asked, "How did you think you did?" I choked. I was holding back tears. I responded, "I think I failed miserably." He replied, "I think you're right." Those words stung like no other in my entire life.

I had failed. My job was on the line. I had two clear choices: I could retreat into an operations role where I had succeeded previously, *or* I could figure out sales. While I originally thought my goal was to reach Director, it was actually to be a successful Director. So, I asked myself, "Have you done everything you possibly can to excel in this role?" Since the answer was no, I decided to get back to work and figure it out. I found Sales 101 courses, certificates, and webinars; I hired a sales confidence coach; and I got a mentor. I did everything I could, and it paid off in the following performance review when I surpassed my sales targets!

Let's step back a bit. Since I arrived in this country, I have been very alert of who I am. I am a Hispanic woman minority. I had the Hispanic saying *calladita te ves más bonita* (a quieter you is a prettier you) engrained in me. I felt that meant I had to be quiet and work harder to fight the stereotypes. My big dream was to be an executive-level leader in a major corporation, inspiring the lives of many along the way. I did not want to jeopardize that in any manner. I kept work and personal separate to be a work-machine, and it worked. I didn't see anything wrong with it. Until I did.

4. When I allowed myself to be me at work…

I started working with a joyful individual who blended the lines between work and personal in a way that connected with everyone. I saw her impact in the work environment; she was creating a culture. People were more relaxed and felt at home. That was leadership magic in its truest form. I wanted to learn from her.

Around this time, I noticed one of my volunteer groups had no direction during an event. No progress was being made. I took the initiative to arrange the work by stations, designate leads, and outline the process. Everyone followed. One of the volunteers, who happened to be the president of a local business, asked me how I was doing. I quickly snapped that I was frustrated. I had to take over for things to get done. It wasn't my role to take, but no one else was doing it! He smiled gently and said, "It is in your nature to be a leader. Embrace it by allowing you to be you." That hit me.

With all this around me, my choices were keeping work versus personal separate *or* learning to have a healthier balance and allowing Jaclyn to be Jaclyn. I chose the latter, which made me happier indeed.

5. When I got to Venice…

I made it happen. My dream to visit Venice came true. My first day, I wept. I was in a gorgeous place, but I had no one to share it with. Traveling alone bothered me. My choices were to let my sadness ruin the trip *or* figure out how to enjoy the adventure. I thought my goal was to visit Venice. I learned that my real goal was to enjoy my visit to Venice. My best friend's advice led me to listen to music and explore Venice. My first step was the gondola ride, where I pushed through my sadness. A picture from that gondola ride is in my office today as a printed reminder that dreams do come true. I need no one other than myself to make it happen.

Many life experiences got me from being a shy child to being a confident leader in business and my community with an amazing support group of friends and family. What worked for me was outlining choices, reminding myself of my goals, and pivoting when needed. The reality is that giving up is always an option, but it's never the choice for those who have goals. Unless you can really say you have done your absolute best, then by all means, walk away to your next goal.

Lastly, I'll share that writing goals is extremely important, so please do it; it is so powerful. I recently found the old Tweety notebook where this once 16-year-old girl wrote her goals for life. The now 40-year-old woman teared up, realizing she had achieved nine of those eleven goals. If I did it, so can you.

A native Venezuelan, Jaclyn came to the United States on a college scholarship. She lives in Missouri with her Tico husband, Carlos. After graduating from high school from Apamates (Maracaibo), she earned a BS in Business Management Systems from Drury University, an MBA from Webster University, and a leadership certificate from the Hispanic Leadership Institute (Class VIII!).

Her career has taken her across industries, including food and beverage, financial institutions, manufacturing, and operations. She is currently the Director of Business Development for Packaging Solutions at DHL Supply Chain and sits on the Contract Packaging Association's Board of Directors.

When asked about her major achievements, she proudly shares how, with her husband's help, they purchased a home for her parents and brother, who live in Venezuela. They moved in last year, and the family is back together after being apart for 23 years! The next step is to grow the family.

Contact information for Jaclyn can be accessed here.

Krysta Grangeno

Breaking the Cycle: Shattering the Silence to Disrupt Generational Trauma

Have you ever cried yourself to sleep, wondering why some children are born into loving, happy families, and you were not? Have you ever looked at others, jealous of the supportive village surrounding them, only to find yourself alone and unsure how to make the most basic connection? These were the questions that plagued my early life as I tried to make sense of being born into a world consumed by violence, abuse, drug addiction, and mental illness, all conditioning me to just survive, never thrive.

In my world, to be quiet was to be safe. To serve was to love and be loved. My first lesson in the safety of silence occurred when I was 6 or 7 years old when a family friend's son sexually assaulted me. As he hid his crime under my bed covers, I dissociated, a technique I honed through experience, despite my young age. I focused on staying still and silent, refusing to make a noise because I knew if caught, I would be beaten. In my young mind, I rationalized that this new abuse was preferable to the physical abuse that I had always known.

My father's family reinforced this illusion of safety in silence. My *abuela* ran her household with iron-clad values and a sharp tongue. She taught us to obediently serve the men while simultaneously telling us,

"Callate la boca!" We quickly learned we only had value if we followed her rules. As I grew, I noticed what happened when we did not. Men were easily forgiven for their drunkenness, violence, and cheating, but the women were brutally iced out if they spoke up or disregarded my Wuela's values. One by one, they would sacrifice their connection with our family until the isolation made them beg forgiveness. In this world, speaking out caused pain and abuse, while silence evaded rejection and isolation.

Alas, the roots of generational trauma were healthy, with me set to become its next victim. But in seventh grade, my English teacher instructed us to memorize the poem "Invictus" by William Ernest Henley. In his words, I found inspiration to control not just my fears, but my life. I could choose a different path, even in the darkest moments. I was, unconsciously at first, resolved to break the cycle. For years, the entire poem resounded in me:

> "Out of the night that covers me,
>> Black as the Pit from pole to pole,
> I thank whatever gods may be
>> For my unconquerable soul.
> In the fell clutch of circumstance
>> I have not winced nor cried aloud.
> Under the bludgeonings of chance
>> My head is bloody, but unbowed.
> Beyond this place of wrath and tears
>> Looms but the Horror of the shade,
> And yet the menace of the years
>> Finds and shall find me unafraid.
> It matters not how strait the gate,
>> How charged with punishments the scroll,
> I am the master of my fate:
>> I am the captain of my soul."

These lines saw me through challenging high school courses, a bachelor's and master's degree, and more traumatic obstacles. They were there every time I cried in despair, wanted to surrender, or endured another panic attack, providing strength when I was weakest. They reminded me that I had the strength to overcome. I had the power to change my life.

And I did, quietly…until Christmas Day 2020.

Through my formative years, I endured visiting my mother in rehab and prison. Her addictions led to her being sentenced to 17 1/2 years the summer after I graduated high school for meth manufacturing and distribution. When she was released early after serving 4 1/2 years, my mother worked hard to repair her relationship with us and set the foundation for long-term sobriety, even moving in with me for a year to take care of me during the worst of my health issues. I was so proud of her. By the time she moved out, I felt I finally had a mother who loved me and could take care of me.

On Christmas that fateful year, my mother called me to tell me she found meth in her house. This started a four-month-long fight to uncover the truth behind her relapse, leading to rehab. I leaned on my social work training and dissociated, finding solace in my favorite coping mechanism. That is until I visited her in rehab.

At that moment, I shattered. The scrubs, slippers, gray walls, and empty promises broke through my dam of repressed emotion. I was instantly transported to the past, reliving the previous prison visits and years of painful memories. As I drove away, I sobbed, tears streaming down my face as my hands trembled on the steering wheel.

When you hit rock bottom, people try to make you feel better by telling you, "There is nowhere to go but up." They lie. I learned there are two pathways:

You can finally give up. Fully give into that sense of emptiness and despair that washes over you. Find peace in the feeling of resignation that overcomes you right before you sleep. Succumb to the thoughts telling you it is fine if you never wake up again and your loved ones will live happily without you,

or

You can fight. With everything inside of you, you break the silence and heal. You latch onto what gives you purpose, no matter how insignificant, and you *fight for it*. You chase away the hopelessness, loneliness, and emptiness that threatens to overwhelm you. You reach into the deepest recesses of your soul and scream, "Not today!"

I did not grasp this in the beginning as unrelenting panic attacks hit me. Waves of memories hit me, paralyzing flashbacks of abuse manifesting as spontaneous panic attacks. Breath shallow, heart racing, my body trembled while the sobs ripped up from my soul, my past traumas crashing over my present. At work and home, indiscriminate, they rolled through my body and left me wrung out. I almost lost everything I loved and worked so hard to create. Through it all, I kept silent the depth of turmoil in my soul and barely told anyone as my world crumbled.

"Not today!"

To live is to rise above. To fall is to remember that I am the master of my fate. I am the captain of my soul.

"Not today!"

I learned that the only way out was through—to break the silence. I had to heal if I had any hope of escaping the demons of my past.

"Not today!"

I had to learn how to thrive.

I have been on this healing journey for four years now. I found the courage to launch two businesses. I found healing and prosperity in reconnecting with my creative spirit. I found help in eye movement desensitization and reprocessing (EMDR) therapy to process the impact of complex trauma, reclaiming my life so I can lead. Professionally, I obtained my life, leadership, and executive coaching certification and transitioned to a position that feeds my soul.

Above all, I have found my voice. Not the voice that advocates and battles injustices—that voice has always been there, guiding me. I am talking about the voice that breaks the silence. The voice that shares my story, that speaks up against generational trauma and destructive conditioning, and models how to thrive. The voice that shares the stages of healing, that shows others that life can get better, and we no longer need to hide.

This voice has ignited a ripple of transformation within my family. Aunts, sisters, and cousins are using their voices to speak out about their trauma, shining light on what was previously unspoken. The instances of domestic violence and abuse by loved ones that were swept under the rug are finally being addressed, even if the perpetrators are rarely punished. Women once ostracized are reconnecting and rebuilding our family. We are there to support each other's journeys, finding community and solidarity among survivors—in more ways than one, we are members of the same family.

We do not always recognize it, but our stories have power—the power to change and the power to connect. Together, we rise above the black tendrils of abuse and create the life of our dreams. Together we reject the residual guilt and shame of our past and harness the lessons and passion to lead. Together we reclaim our space and value in this world and finally break the cycle.

Together, we become *calladitas rising*.

Meet Krysta Grangeno, a trailblazer driven by a passion for authenticity, empowerment, and values. With a Bachelor's in Social Work in hand, Krysta wasted no time diving into a community organizing internship through the Center for Community Change. Following graduation, she wholeheartedly embraced her role in the local affiliate of the Gamaliel Network, collaborating with church leaders to build bridges with immigrant communities, develop leaders, and influence national-level policies. Recognizing that long-lasting change requires a profound understanding of one's self and organizational systems, Krysta pursued and achieved her Master's in Nonprofit Management and ICF Certification as a Life, Leadership, and Executive Coach.

In her roles as an Operations Director, Chief of Staff, Sr. Manager of Statewide Initiatives, and Leadership coach, Krysta proves she is dedicated to making a difference in the lives of others. Her expertise extends to facilitating focus groups and leadership programs, operations, DEI (diversity, equity, and inclusion), and program development. Through these endeavors, she tirelessly advocates for systemic change, addressing inequities, and creating opportunities for people to shine.

Annalisa Hernandez

Faith Moves Mountains:
A Testimony with a Twist

According to Matthew 17:20 (NLT), Jesus said, "You don't have enough faith. I tell you the truth, if you had faith even as small as a mustard seed, you could say to this mountain, 'Move from here to there,' and it would move. Nothing would be impossible."

I never quite understood this verse until God decided to move my mountain, which came in the form of a toxic coworker. In our family and culture, women are often told to be quiet, challenged by their male counterparts to remain silent. Yet, as Christians, when God prompts us to speak up, we must be obedient.

I hadn't shared this testimony widely before, save for a few coworkers, my family, and a handful of friends who've also navigated toxic work environments. I've likened it to a "living hell" more than an "environment."

Early in my military career, I learned the phrase, "Shut up and color," which means to be quiet and do what you are told. When you are new on staff, you start at the bottom, hoping a new recruit will soon replace you as the rookie. After seven PCS (Permanent Change of Station) or reassignments, I learned to make the best of challenging environments, regardless of bad morale or unpleasant locations.

In the military, you cannot just quit with two weeks' notice, nor is it easy to relocate or change career fields. Early on, a supervisor told me that if you are dissatisfied with your military career, remember that change will come from changing your job (cross-train), location, or the people around you. If you manage to get one assignment with an amazing job in an amazing location, and with incredible staff, consider yourself truly blessed.

I don't remember how the "living hell" started, but I certainly remember how it ended. At one point, four of us were desperately seeking ways to transfer or change career fields by cross-training to escape a specific toxic coworker. One new staff member, within two years, was already trying to cross-train out of our career field.

This toxic coworker brought a level of corruption that made the rest of us fear being around him, especially when something might set him off. He was perpetually negative and usually in a bad mood. We shared office space, and I kept a notebook tally of his negative behavior during phone calls. Eventually, I realized how ridiculous and futile this was.

As my superior, I had to follow his instructions, provided they were not illegal, unethical, or immoral. So, I did the "shut up and color" yet venting everything in therapy sessions. After two and a half years in this stressful environment and daily prayer, I took a different approach, unknowingly taking the first step for God to move my mountain.

After a brief phone conversation with my mom about my strenuous work week, she asked if I had ever anointed myself and my workspace. Until then, I had only anointed myself. At my next opportunity, alone in the office, I did what needed to be done and hoped God would handle the rest.

Armed with a small bottle of anointing oil given to me by a friend, I prayed over the office space, anointing the chairs, computer mouse, monitor, keyboards, desk phone, and door frame. I prayed for peace and for anything not of God to leave our workspace.

By the end of the week, I noticed my toxic coworker packing up his personal items at his desk. He calmly told me he was moving across the hall, which was a smaller space than he and I were sharing. Moments later, another coworker, whose office he was moving into, approached me with concern and looked upset. My immediate reaction of laughter and relief left him confused. I explained what I had done with my office space and suggested he could do the same.

Within two weeks, our toxic coworker moved to a different building down the street. About a year later, he was reassigned to a whole other state. Our prayers had finally been answered. God had moved my mountain 621 miles away. Hallelujah!

In the days leading up to his departure, I felt compelled to speak to him about his eternal status. Despite my reluctance, I knew obedience to God was necessary. Three days before his last day at work, I finally approached him, asking, "If you were to die tomorrow, do you know where you would spend eternity?" After a pause, he assured me he knew. He thanked me for taking the time to speak to him, as he could see it was a difficult conversation for me. With a sigh, I left his office feeling as if a weight lifted off me.

Six months after he moved out of state, I received an email from him. My stomach clenched at the sight of his name. In his email, he explained his behavior stemmed from trauma experienced during past deployments and apologized for how he treated me. He noted I was one of three staff members who showed him kindness despite his actions. He stated that he hoped for forgiveness and understood if I never replied. Eventually I forgave him, yet I never replied to his email.

This experience reminds me of another Bible verse, 2 Timothy 1:7: "God has not given us a spirit of fear and timidity, but of power, love, and self-discipline." Our family, culture, and coworkers might try to silence us, but when God ordains us to speak, we must be obedient.

Annalisa Hernandez, based in Stockdale, Texas, draws inspiration from her deep-rooted faith, close-knit family, and 22 years of military service. Growing up in a military family, she embraced responsibility as the oldest sibling, a value she now weaves into her encouraging stories. Annalisa's writing is known for its relatability and humor, offering readers a perfect blend of inspiration and laughter.

Annalisa enjoys spending quality time with her family, working on DIY projects, and deepening her faith. Her love for Texas and its vibrant culture shines through in her writing, making her books a true reflection of her life and values. A recent accomplishment she cherishes is helping her dad build a house, proof of her hands-on approach to life.

She finds solace and motivation in Philippians 4:13, "I can do all things through Christ who strengthens me," a verse that resonates deeply in her journey as a writer and beyond. Whether you're a fan of rom-coms or just in need of a good laugh, Annalisa Hernandez's novels are a perfect escape for anyone looking for a feel-good read.

Suzy Barbosa

The Voices Within

My name is Suzy Barbosa. I am an immigrant from Brazil and the firstborn of four siblings. Being the eldest sister implied some responsibilities and duties. Responsibilities made me the "protector" of the younger ones. I was a protector who looked after them with love and encouraged them to have a better attitude, to eat well, and to be on time. I entertained them to see them smiling at my childhood silly ideas and tricks. I felt privileged to be the oldest of the siblings because they listened to me. My voice mattered. They didn't always listen, but if they were in trouble, they came running after me. I was a big sister and a friend to lean on. I learned to be patient and let them be themselves.

My memories include us sitting in the kitchen sharing stories. We learned early to be together and deal with surprises. Among the many happy memories I have from my childhood is my grandmother reading Bible stories to us. She had a tremendous impact on us as she helped us discover a love of reading. A story found in Mark 5:41 that always caught my attention was about a little girl healed by Jesus. He resurrected her and said to her: "*Talitha cumi,*" which means: "Girl, I tell you: get up." in Aramaic and Portuguese: "*Levanta-te!*" This word has resonated with me throughout many experiences in my life. It gave me the confidence not to accept defeat but to honor courage and move forward in life. I later discovered through conversation with my sisters that we shared a similar experience. We always remember these stories and apply them to our own lives.

I was 15 years old when my parents divorced. The entire family felt the impact. At the time, the youngest child was only 4 years old. Going through this complex experience, I knew that my youngest sister was the most affected by this situation. She was a very rebellious, impatient, and sensitive kid.

As we embraced challenges, both sisters looked to me for leadership and guidance. I have always been a good student and a very active member of the community. As a highly performing kid at home and beyond, I enjoyed getting involved by playing sports, singing in the choir, collecting donations for the church, or simply going out with other friends for school projects. Life has always been so interesting to me, and I wanted to explore more. I believe it was my purpose to inspire and support them. Growing up together was never boring. We created our bonds through caring, strength, and solidarity.

Due to circumstances out of our control, our parents went in different directions. Our grandpa passed away. Again, our lives were torn apart, leaving us in different circumstances, different cities, and far from the people we loved. At a time of no internet access or video calls, I know we missed being together.

For many years, the family faced resentment, disagreements, physical threats, and psychological abuse. We were tired of being too passive and obeying the rules. The loss of our grandmother made things even worse for us. For many years she had been our protector. Now we had to decide what to do with our lives. The pressure of dealing with our parents' divorce created trauma, stress, and anxiety and affected our emotional well-being.

When we met again, I was going to college, my youngest sister was pregnant, and my middle sister started her first job. My younger sister came to me. She shared her emotions about getting pregnant at a young age. I heard her. During our conversation, we recalled the story of Talitha, which brought meaning to our suffering by reminding us that we can pick ourselves up and move forward despite life's challenges. Rising was an arduous process of personal growth for each of us. We often found ourselves seemingly overwhelmed by bitterness, fears, and difficulties.

What I learned from our meeting was that being quiet could never symbolize peace or happiness. As young people confronting adult challenges prematurely, our parents were no longer available. We had to learn how to fight for our lives and achieve our rights and our happiness. We encouraged each other to move forward in life.

I remember meeting my younger sister many times. She shared a moment on a bus, sitting next to the driver. On the driver's radio, someone was reflecting on the passage in Mark 5:41. She felt it was a message intended for her. My sister was feeling abandoned, looking for strength to move on. Imagine a young pregnant woman unaccompanied in a society that demands youth, wealth, and social well-being. Think about an immense burden that forces you to choose between studying and raising a child. This burden is too great for many young women. I couldn't find the words to condemn her. Instead, I recognized the critical need for support and friendship for a young woman in such a vulnerable position. We hugged.

That day we met, she came to announce the birth of my first niece, asked me to choose a name, and told me that our middle sister would be the godmother. This vulnerable young girl had a plan. I was scared for her, but I did not tell her. I was trying to show bravery, as an oldest sister is expected to do. However, in my heart, I was not sure of the vision. I was doubtful that my sister would be able to accomplish this mission. I was wrong. She was determined to confront cultural expectations, fight the status quo, and resist anyone's negative opinions. I never imagined she had that degree of maturity!

During these difficult times, my middle sister and I concentrated our efforts to support our younger sister, offering whatever help we could. Despite her strong and fighting nature, she was afraid but proved to be a fighter. She considered me an older sister and a confidant, but she taught me the true meaning of courage and determination. She left this world during the pandemic in 2021. My middle sister was there being a comfort to her as our world fell apart with this horrible death. From a young age, my younger sister struggled for acceptance and understanding. In our large community, where addressing teen pregnancy is challenging, we feel a responsibility to break the cycle of defeat and build community support for young mothers.

For many years, I closely followed community projects that were raising awareness about the impact of teenage pregnancy, in particular the work of the *Pastoral da Criança* in Brazil, offering an incredible program that works in the areas of health, nutrition, community education, and prevention of violence within families and schools. Offering support to young people at this stage is essential. Also, I was part of the youth ministry in my church, helping young people to find a sense of purpose. We had retreats, conferences, and one-on-one meetings with young girls who were in search of a better life. These experiences helped me as well to deal with my internal conflicts and encouraged me to deepen my relationship with God and find even deeper meaning for my life.

Early in life I was advocating for my younger siblings. From my sisters, I learned how to share my true story. With nothing left to hide or lose, my sisters were the first to know my emotions. When we were together, we would ask for advice and encouragement. We had our own conflicts. From my sisters, I learned how to stay true to my own identity and aspirations. I made my voice heard. I learned to accept criticism but to resist when necessary. They taught me to be the protagonist of my life, shaping the path toward who I want to be. I gave voice to my desires and was never afraid to walk alone. Despite the geographical distance, we decided to remain strong and united. I am grateful to my sisters, who inspire me to become the best version of myself. I can't think of anyone who could impact you more than your siblings. My sisters became the voices within.

Sisterhood teaches us how to use our own voices. It makes us fight back when there is no one to fight for us. It teaches us to be protagonists and continue climbing mountains if necessary to achieve our goals. I want to "end" this story of sisterhood with this quote from Latina Claudia Romo: "Lead like a mother: Don't underestimate the power of maternal instincts in leadership." Yes!

Don't be afraid to make mistakes. Our personal journey doesn't have to be perfect. What we need is to be authentic. Set boundaries and let others know your expectations. Learn to say no to the destructive voices inside you. Seek professional help when possible and feed your faith. This is your most extraordinary strength that no one can take away from you.

Talitha cumi! Levanta-te!

Suzy Barbosa is a Latina from Brazil. She serves as Community and Business Development Coordinator for the International Institute, where she supports immigrant entrepreneurs through business development and consulting. After relocating to the U.S. in 2009, Suzy's journey led her to be nominated for the G.R.I.T. community in 2023, contributing to the *Intention: Deconstructing G.R.I.T. Collection* with her story as an Amazonian woman. She collaborates with nonprofits like Viva Brasil STL and the Hispanic Leaders Group of Greater St. Louis. Suzy is a team leader of the Brazilian Women's Leadership Group, working with the Brazilian Consulate in Chicago and other organizations. An advocate for small business growth and economic inclusion, she has partnered with leaders to enhance STL's business ecosystem. She holds an associate degree from St. Louis Community College-Meramec and a bachelor's degree from Webster University. Outside work, Suzy enjoys nature, reading, gardening, singing, and family time with her husband, Patrick, and their son Joe.

Contact information for Suzy can be accessed here.

Nerishka Cruz De La Rosa

I Did It, and So Can You!

It all started when I was 18. I was a teenager figuring out my future while trying to exceed expectations from my parents and society. I am the youngest of three; my oldest brother was starting a family while the middle brother was studying biology to become a doctor. Then it was me, not knowing what I wanted, running out of time, and feeling overwhelmed. I have always seen my parents and brothers accomplishing everything in life and succeeding in their jobs and responsibilities. When you idolize a perfect family structure—a financially providing father and a multitasking mother—you often feel compelled to prove your worth to those you love. I always wanted to follow in the footsteps of my parents and brothers.

I am not close to my mom's side of the family, except for my Titi and Tio, whom I see often and who are constant supporters. I grew up closer to my dad's side because they held more family gatherings and holidays. I cherished those family times and childhood memories. However, as an adult, I realized their behavior and judgment had a significant impact on me. I cared deeply about their opinions yet felt unable to respond or defend myself out of respect for elders, instilled by my parents' emphasis on obedience. This was a pattern deeply inherent in our family dynamics. Breaking free from toxic cycles often requires confronting our own imperfections.

College approached, and with volleyball scholarships in hand, I chose to stay close to my parents by attending their alma mater and where they fell in love. Chemistry seemed like the path to success, but my lack of interest in the subject quickly became evident. Failing my first semester, I felt lost and unmotivated. What would they tell the family and friends? Which "successful" career would I switch to? Do I even want to continue my education? A heated Mother's Day argument with my dad brought his disappointment to the surface. He articulated what everyone was thinking but feared to voice aloud. The words remain vivid just as if it happened yesterday. It was a bittersweet reality check, but I'm grateful for the breaking point. It forced me to make one of the toughest decisions of my life.

I'm unsure how I coordinated a new plan by myself at a new college in New York. Moving to a place I had never visited before or even knowing the language, which I didn't dominate at all, was not an easy choice, but was necessary. Hospitality Management with a minor in Culinary Arts, along with volleyball, was my new dream. The hardest part was envisioning a future without my best friend, who'd been my rock for over 15 years. We'd always dreamed of sharing a dorm room for the next four years. Despite the fear of her reaction, I was immensely grateful for her love and support as I shared my plan to pursue my dreams in the U.S. and escape the disappointment of my family.

The day of departure finally arrived. I packed one suitcase with a plaid design and various shades of pink. It was a gift from my godmother, along with a cozy black coat that remains with me. My mom and my brother traveled with me, left me at the dorms, and went back without knowing that it was my last time ever coming back home. At 18, leaving home was the toughest decision I've ever made. With no clear path ahead, I embarked on a solo journey filled with fear and uncertainty. Yet, this experience taught me self-confidence and resilience. I know my family doubted me at that moment. I did too. Rock bottom forced me to confront my reality. I needed a change and a challenge to prove not just to my family but to myself my own worth. My story starts there, fueled by the resentment of failure and the desperate hope for a new beginning.

During my junior year, I fell in love. After a year of dating, we moved in together. Though struggling financially, our love grew, and we moved to St. Louis in 2018. I moved out of love, not driven by a desire to call St. Louis home. Difficulties arose as we navigated external challenges and struggled to set boundaries and prioritize our family. Beyond that, we pursued our love for seven years before we welcomed a baby girl into our home. Motherhood has been a profound joy, fulfilling my life in ways I never imagined. On the surface, I had everything, including a beautiful home, a stable job, and an amazing little family. Inside, I was breaking. My relationship was not what it needed, or I wanted it, to be.

My attempt to avoid conflict kept the relationship going externally, but it was slowly breaking me. The genuine and real connection we once shared was fading away, seemingly beyond our control. It felt like a dam about to burst; a big crash was unavoidable. A part of growing up is accepting that sometimes you outgrow the people you love, even if it hurts. Life's experiences had changed us. It wasn't anyone's fault; change is inevitable. We simply didn't share the same values, dreams, and priorities anymore. Exhausted and heartbroken from fighting alone, a simple question destroyed the illusion and hope. With a heavy heart but immense courage, I knew it was time to walk away, to do it again for myself.

The first six months were brutal. Accepting my new reality while raising my daughter as a single mom brought waves of grief and loneliness. The guilt of disrupting my daughter's life was, and still is, a heavy weight. There was a realization of a new identity. This brought mourning of lost memories and an uncertain future. The power to navigate life and responsibilities while healing and grieving was met with a sadness of human pettiness and the feeling of shame. I distanced myself from places, hobbies, and people associated with the past. I knew I lost time that I would never get back. However, I realized I had to channel that pain into something positive. In that moment, I knew I had to find myself again.

My focus became my jobs, my business, and most importantly, my daughter. Slowly, I navigated the heartbreak, finding peace and stability in prioritizing my daughter's well-being. I started to regain my shine and true colors day by day. Suddenly, two years passed, and I was thriving! I've achieved a sense of balance in my professional career, single motherhood, business, and personal life. A supportive network of new friends emerged. I embraced the modeling journey and launched my "Cool Mom" Instagram page. I pursued new challenges at work, proving my tenacity. Most importantly, I started to prioritize myself. I found peace, a peace I never thought possible before.

Two years of accomplishment and change...imagine what could happen in 10?

The 18-year-old boarding that plane lost and scared would have been proud of the woman and mother who wiped her tears and made it happen, regardless of the doubt and the judgment. I am grateful for every laugh, every tear, and every part of my past, as it has forged my strength and courage. I've stumbled and fallen many times but always found the resilience to rise again. No longer bound by fear or the expectations of others, I refuse to pause my aspirations for anyone else. I've learned to define my worth and recognize my place in the world. My brilliance may intimidate some, but I've discovered unwavering courage within myself.

To my dear daughter, I hope she knows her inherent value and worth. May she navigate a world free from societal labels, where success is defined by her unique journey. I want her to be a thriving professional, a loving mother, a confident woman—or anything else she desires.

I want every woman to know that you have the strength to walk away from anything that no longer serves you. A place, a relationship, a job—it doesn't matter. There's power in making difficult decisions, even if they're painful. When something doesn't align with your values or fails to bring you fulfillment, prioritize yourself and your needs. Every woman deserves a life filled with joy, respect, and acceptance, even if it means walking alone.

Embrace life without hesitation, fear, or doubt. Never settle for less than you deserve. Chase your dreams relentlessly, defend your values fiercely, and prioritize your well-being above all else. Remember, every decision shapes your future, and even mistakes are stepping stones to something extraordinary. You can still achieve your dreams after becoming a mother, weathering a breakup, or experiencing life's inevitable changes. There will be times when walking away feels scary and dark, but trust me, my love…

I did it, and so can you.

My name is Nerishka Cruz De La Rosa, and this is my story.

Born and raised in Puerto Rico, Nerishka Cruz De La Rosa was the youngest and only girl among three siblings. At 18, with a passion for volleyball and culinary arts, she packed her bags and headed to New York to pursue her dreams. After a challenging but rewarding career path, she began her journey in the hospitality industry.

Landing in St. Louis in 2018, Nerishka served as a Program Coordinator at the Hispanic Chamber of Commerce. There, she thrived in a supportive community. Today, she oversees the St. Louis branch of Hospitality Staffing Solutions, where she connects applicants and clients to strengthen the region's workforce development.

Beyond work, Nerishka is a proud mom to a bright and happy 3-year-old who loves to eat rice and play with puppies! In her free time, Nerishka runs her "Hecho en Casa" business and occasionally participates in fun fundraising modeling events.

Contact information for Nerishka can be accessed here.

Francelly Rosas

Persevering Through Different Seasons of Life

Resilient Roots

My story starts in Mayaguez, Puerto Rico, born to hard-working parents, Julia and Frank. My dad completed a third-grade education, just enough to learn how to write and do math before my grandpa took him out of school to work and help the family. My mom was able to go to high school but never finished because of the same reasons; at 16, she went to work with one of her sisters to get money for her family. From wanting to become an engineer, my dad gave up on that dream when he couldn't go to school. However, his new dream of becoming a business owner came true after many years of learning from others. Later in their lives, my mom and dad met and started their family.

I was born in 1992, the youngest of two sisters. My parents sent me to private school, which was a great privilege at the time, and took a lot of their efforts to afford it. At the age of 6, I experienced my first category 4 hurricane, George. It came full swing, destroying my house. I remember vividly how the roof of our wooden house flew away, how our furniture and beds got wet, and how my parents fell down the stairs trying to rescue some of the items. Witnessing this at an early age made me appreciate my parents so much as I got to see how hard it was for them to recover the material things but never lose sight of the most important things, which were family, unity, and health.

In school, I was the nerd. I knew I needed to be a good kid, study hard, and get good grades so I would earn my parents' pride and appreciation. Being the nerd, I was also very shy. All I did was smile and laugh at others' jokes so I wouldn't be mocked, with a desire to make new friends. It all changed when my older sister entered high school. She gave me the confidence I needed to break the shell of shyness and start building genuine friendships.

Influencers

The first influencer in my life and someone who shaped me was my big sister, Leslie. Growing up with a big sister was another privilege in my life. She was there when I had my first period, she taught me about fashion, and she developed my taste for music in English. She also taught me how to use a computer for the first time, how to navigate the internet, and to open my first social media account; yes, it was MySpace. My sister was the rebel. She was not afraid of speaking up, even if that cost her a fight with my parents. My parents were older and very strict. They loved and cared for us. Sometimes they gave us tough love, didn't listen, and it had to be their way. Being the obedient one, I always paid attention to these fights between my sister and my parents so I would avoid having these in the future. What I didn't know was that would eventually translate into staying quiet to avoid conflict and debate. As an adult, I realized how many unhealthy patterns we lived through but that we somehow normalized them. Unhealthy patterns included non-confrontation, taboo topics, one-sided conversations because someone is always right, and an unwillingness to change. I am grateful for my sister. Through her, I learned that being a rebel and speaking up does not mean that you are a bad person. Speaking up when it's fair challenges people's mindsets and behaviors, eventually making a change.

Discovering Era

My twenties were significant and certainly molded the woman I am today. In college, my personality fully developed. I learned about love and heartbreak, experienced a big loss, and went through a world pandemic.

As any other young kid graduating high school, I had an idea of what I wanted to be when I grew up but was never sure. At some point, I wanted to become what my father couldn't and become an engineer. I changed my mind and went for business with the dream of becoming a business owner like my dad. I truly enjoyed serving people and offering my services; my dad was always my inspiration. With that in mind, I went to business school and, again, was a nerd. In my third year, I realized that only having good grades would not take me far, so I started to get out of my comfort zone, taking on leadership roles within the school, which led me to get an internship. I never imagined or wished to leave Puerto Rico. I thought I would graduate and stay close to family, but the unexpected happened. One big corporation came to the campus to recruit, and I was one of the lucky students selected to travel to St. Louis, Missouri, to complete a summer internship. When that happened, my life changed completely. I took a leap of faith and accepted this opportunity, even with my fear of never leaving the comfort of my home and my broken English. To this day, I describe this as the most courageous moment in my life because I did it with fear. I was not 100 percent confident I could do it, but I still embraced the opportunity that knocked at my door. The internship eventually became my full-time job, and I embraced a life far from my homeland.

The same year I was getting ready to leave my family in Puerto Rico, my dad was diagnosed with cancer, and our world crumbled. Seeing him trying to battle cancer will always be the saddest memory of all, but also the truest example of resilience. He kept his spirits up and remained positive even to his last day. While this has been the most devastating moment in my life, it also showed me the strength and faith that live in me. My dad will always live through me in everything I do and every person I connect with. I have his grit, determination, and courage.

After my dad's passing, I started dating the man that would become my husband. He showed up at the right time. Being taught to be an independent woman, sometimes we become rough and build a wall that makes it harder to fully give ourselves to someone. With him, I learned to become more patient, to be softer with my words, to be a better listener, and to ask and accept help when needed. Thanks to him, I have become a better leader in my life and profession. He is another influencer in my life.

Adulting

Fast forward, I am in my adulting era, where my focus is staying true to myself, getting the fierce leader to come out and conquer the world with love and kindness. Adulting seems so desirable when we are kids or teenagers. As an adult, I wish I could go back and experience the life of a kid one more time. As Latinas, we are molded to work harder than others and not speak a lot about our accomplishments so we don't come off as arrogant. I come from a household where a job was appreciated, and we had to be grateful for it. We learn not to complain because you would get in trouble and get fired. I've gone through those "rules" and it did not work out. We cannot expect others to guess how we feel and do something for us if we do not speak up. Change does not come when you stay quiet, but change happens when you speak up, and that goes for everything.

There is a time to speak up, and there is a time to listen. You can be loving and kind, yet you can be a fierce and assertive leader. The key is to show respect and appreciation and learn to listen, providing a safe space for others to come forward with their real perspectives. Throughout my life, I have learned that there is nothing more beautiful than someone who is real and authentic. Authenticity is noticed when you can see someone's vulnerability, acknowledging their mistakes and taking ownership to better themselves. There is great power in that.

We have hurricanes, heat waves, and tropical breezes in Puerto Rico. I like to use that as a metaphor for life. We have times in our lives that are comparable to hurricanes—turbulent and destructive. These are times that break us and leave us in pieces. We also have times of heat waves, where we go through emotions of fear, insecurity, and rage. Lastly, we have times when we feel the breeze with calm and blissful moments. You will have them all in your life. There are seasons of fear of the unknown. There are seasons of prosperity, but behind it all, there is always hope, love, and kindness in different shapes and forms.

Francelly Rosas is a young business professional originally from Maya-guez, Puerto Rico. She has a business degree from the University of Puerto Rico-Mayaguez. Francelly has built a career with The Boeing Company, having fulfilled several roles in different business functions, including pro-curement, financial analysis, chief of staff, and user experience. In her spare time, Francelly enjoys mentoring and helping others with their resumes and in any capacity she can. She has served in different leadership roles for the Boeing Latino Business Resource Group, including local chapter chair and Enterprise Global Strategy Lead. Additionally, Francelly is an active member of the Association of Latino Professionals for America (ALPFA). Her leadership has earned her several recognitions.

Contact information for Francelly can be accessed here.

Elisa Bender

Blindsided

Blindsided! I always thought of myself as intuitive…always trusting my gut. I knew myself and listened to my body. In January 2017—my world stopped. I had a choice to let it break me or to get my world spinning again. Determined to not give up hope, I chose to be inspired. I became driven to make a positive impact on my community and within my culture.

A love and appreciation for my Hispanic heritage and community was instilled in me from the day I was born. Raised in St. Louis, I grew up a dancer and had a passion for the arts. Proudly, I am the daughter of an immigrant. My mother kicked down doors for her community, stood up to those that discriminated, and laid a foundation for the future of Hispanics in St Louis. She is an icon in the Hispanic community. I fell in love with a great guy who is my rock, who helps and supports my ideas and crazy schedule. We have two strong kids who bring us so much joy. Both have grown into fantastic young adults who lead with their hearts, showing compassion, caring, and kindness for all people. As a result of the love, upbringing, and support I have received, I became inspired to be an advocate for our Hispanic arts, culture, and community through the Hispanic Festival, Inc. organization, a nonprofit my mom started.

Monday morning, January 2, 2017, I received a phone call that changed my life. I had been diagnosed with breast cancer. No warning, no lump, no symptoms. My doctor instructed me to get a routine mammogram. Throughout my life, I have been very diligent about following doctor's orders and staying on top of my health. There was no reason to suspect anything was wrong when I went to the examination. Then the phone call came, followed by shock and disbelief. The mental and physical fear that went through me was palpable. I had no idea what I was up against, what the treatment plan was, or what recovery would be like. Would I even make it? Although there was an unknown and that phone call changed my life, there was a determination to approach this with the mantra that "it's just a bump in the road." I did my best to maintain that mindset throughout the ups and downs of battling cancer.

With support from my husband and family, we chose a team of doctors who laid out the treatment plan: lumpectomy, chemotherapy, and radiation. The next six months were exhausting—mentally, spiritually, and physically.

In the beginning, it did not seem real. I felt great. The hardest part in the early stages of treatment was trying to accept and get my head around what was about to happen, including losing my hair (and I *love* my long, thick hair). My life was about to be put into the hands of doctors I had just met. The kids were young and needed a strong role model. Putting a lot of pressure on myself, I was trying to keep life as normal as possible. All of this took an emotional toll.

My relationship with God became stronger as I prayed all the time. I asked God to be with my family as I went through treatment and to help keep me safe. I talked to my aunt and brother, who had passed, and asked them to talk to God, also.

The entire process was physically draining as I started off with a lumpectomy, which was, thankfully, successful. The next treatment step was chemotherapy, and it kicked my butt in both a good and bad way. I had four rounds of chemo, with one every three weeks. The chemotherapy made me very sick for about 10 days; then, for the next 10 days, I would feel better and go back to work. This lasted for several months. During this time, I had a lot of time to reflect.

My husband or mom would stay with me for a few days after each chemotherapy session when I felt the worst. As I started to feel better in the chemo cycle, I would be home by myself in bed. I enjoyed this time being by myself, as I am pretty introverted and love the quiet.

As I lay in bed recuperating, I thought about all the things I wanted to do once this bump in the road was defeated. There were many things that I had wanted to do in the past but felt I had the time to accomplish. The idea of "time" changed with my diagnosis. I needed to get this treatment done so I could put it behind me and get to the things that I always thought I had "time" to do.

During these quiet moments to myself, I thought about my family and the future. I thought about the dream vacations I wanted to take with my husband and kids. I thought about the different ideas I had that would bring attention to the Hispanic arts and community. I thought about the endless opportunities and possibilities for my Hispanic community. All these ideas and dreams I had put on the side. Life was just passing me by. I truly believed God had a plan for me. This push was exactly what I needed to propel me toward the new path and take action. I was a productive member of the community, but I had so much more to give and do.

I continued my treatment and finally finished at the end of July 2017. I made it over the bump in the road. Once I was done, I put every piece of the past six months away: boxed up, trashed, given away, out of my head. I did not want to reflect on what I just went through. There would be no dwelling. I wanted to look forward, not back.

The journey to recovery from the cancer diagnosis was no easy task. I had to consistently remind myself of the end goal: get through treatment. Then it was time to live life to the fullest. Say yes. Begin now. Just start. Make the jump. Fortunately, I had a strong role model who always did just that. I was able to observe and absorb information as my mom helped build a road for me and so many in the Hispanic community. I was going to be able to stand on her shoulders and make the impact I was wanting to make. It was my time to begin.

In August 2017, I ran the idea of organizing a Hispanic artist meetup with a local cultural institution. They offered to host the first meeting. In October 2017, it started with a post on social media inviting artists to attend. In order to ensure the success of that first meeting, I reached out to people I did not know but knew they were artists in some medium. I had no real agenda. I just jumped. It was terrifying, but I remember calling my husband on the way to the meeting and asking him what if no one showed up. He has been and always will be one of my biggest supporters. He said even if it's just you and one other person that shows up, it's a start and a success—the unknown is the scariest part. You have to just begin…jump.

This meeting was the start of an incredible opportunity and future for the Hispanic arts in St Louis. Over 15 people attended, most of whom I did not know. I met and connected with people who shared the same goals and passion for our arts community. We eventually formed a nonprofit, Latinx Arts Network. Through this organization, we have been able to elevate and organize our Hispanic artist community. A few of the accomplishments include starting an online artist directory, creating the Building Bridges mural on the Delmar Loop, starting the Latinx Film

Festival, creating an annual art exhibit, and our biggest initiative yet, collaborating on the first-ever Hispanic Heritage Flag.

Fair or unfair, unexpected events happen to all of us. The key is how we respond to life's unexpected events. It's what we do because of or in spite of these events that can help us excel and broaden our impact. Don't take life for granted. Don't keep putting off your dreams and ambitions. Trust in yourself and the journey ahead. Allow passion to fuel you. Take the leap with confidence.

Elisa Bender, a first-generation Hispanic American of Bolivian descent, is a passionate advocate for the Hispanic arts, culture, and community. She has received talent and academic scholarships, performed as a St. Louis Rams Cheerleader, and taught Hispanic dance at various events.

Elisa is actively involved in the Hispanic community, serving on the board of the Hispanic Festival, Inc., and co-founder of the Latinx Arts Network. She holds two bachelor's degrees from Lindenwood University, works for a large corporation, and co-owns a Homeowners Association management company with her husband. Elisa also serves on the board for the St. Louis Visionary Awards.

A breast cancer survivor, Elisa enjoys family time with her husband and their two children, movies, volunteering, and reading. She credits her mother, Haniny, as her mentor and has been inspired by Haniny to cherish her roots, embrace diversity, and strive for personal excellence.

Contact information for Elisa can be accessed here.

Josephine "Josie" Santana

From Silence to Strength: Finding My Voice as a "No Sabo" Kid

Growing up as a "No Sabo" kid was filled with confusion, identity struggles, and a deep sense of not belonging. As a mixed Latina in Chicago, I was surrounded by Hispanic diversity; the language, food, and customs were everywhere. Despite being immersed in the vibrant culture, there was always a barrier that made me feel like I didn't fit in. I'm the second generation of Mexican and Puerto Rican descent. Being raised in America, English was spoken in our household. I only had one grandparent who didn't speak fluent English, but she understood it, and we could communicate. The need to learn or speak Spanish was less important. While I enjoyed eating the food and listening to the music, I didn't participate in my culture's customs or deep-rooted traditions. My light skin set me apart even more; I didn't fit the "browned-skinned" image of what a Hispanic should look like. This physical difference and my inability to speak Spanish made it hard to find my place, especially in a community where I felt like an outsider.

The term "No Sabo" is a label given to Hispanics who cannot speak the language. It was a label that stuck and reminded me that I didn't fit in. I was called this by strangers, friends, and family members. My inability to speak Spanish was seen as a failure, amplifying my insecurities and furthering my self-doubt. It was a harsh reminder that I was different. The hurt of being called "No Sabo" cut deep, where my lack of fluency was a source of jokes, ridicule, and scorn. Relatives would make snide remarks or shake their heads in disbelief, deepening these feelings of inadequacy and isolation. What hurt the most wasn't my inability to speak Spanish or the mockery that followed; it was about being disconnected from the people I was supposed to be closest to. I wanted so much to engage in conversations, laugh at jokes, and experience all the things about my culture that I couldn't understand; my self-doubt held me back, and I lacked the confidence to be fully present. Not only did they keep me from speaking around other Hispanics, but they also made me lack the confidence to speak in general. My natural shyness and introverted personality compounded these feelings of meagerness.

My identity struggles transcended beyond family. In school, I couldn't fit in with Hispanic kids who spoke fluent Spanish, and I wasn't able to fit in with the non-Hispanic either. Not only was I unable to speak Spanish, but my English vocabulary was limited. I found it challenging to find the right words to express myself. I was caught between two worlds, unable to connect to either. I felt like I didn't have a voice and unsafe to assert myself or my opinions. Keeping quiet, I feared that my lack of fluency and cultural knowledge would make me out to be an impostor, undeserving of claiming any part of my culture. In my community, Spanish is spoken just as much as English is. The community events, festivals, and cultural celebrations felt foreign and intimidating. While they should have felt familial, my lack of fluency was met with frustration and ridicule. My authenticity as a Spanish person was questioned because I needed to fit the expectations of what a Hispanic person should be. Meanwhile, non-Hispanics made stereotypical assumptions about my background without even knowing who I was.

As I got older, I continued to grapple with my identity, struggling to find a place I could belong. Joining the military gave me a unique opportunity to address my issues. I couldn't hide my ethnicity. The ethnic origin of "Latin American" is shown on my records for leaders to see; my distinctively Spanish last name is worn boldly and proudly on my uniform, and my curvy physique and curly hair are on display. I was stereotyped by peers, superiors, and colleagues because they judged me based on what they saw rather than what they knew. They'd make backhanded comments, racist innuendos, or perceive me as less than. I constantly questioned why I was subject to these prejudices, especially when I didn't even speak the language or was fully immersed in the culture. On the outside, looking in, I was undoubtedly Hispanic, but on the inside, I still felt like I didn't belong to the culture I was perceived to represent. I felt alone, misunderstood, and unsure if I was worthy enough to speak up. I didn't want to be portrayed as the feisty Latina or let my capabilities be questioned based on stereotypes rather than my actual performance. I constantly needed to prove myself. My determination to excel fueled me. I pushed myself harder to prove to everyone, but most importantly, myself, that I was more than my perceived shortcomings.

The military tested my resilience and enabled me to find my voice. Others saw me through their narrow lenses. They didn't care about my internal struggles. They saw a Hispanic woman and judged me. Both painful and empowering, I was forced to face the fact that regardless of my own insecurities, I represented my Hispanic community. My actions, successes, and even failures reflect them, and I had a duty to represent them well.

I began to look at things from a different perspective. As the leader I aspired to be, I used this to challenge cultural stereotypes and redefine what it means to be Hispanic. I learned I didn't have to fit society's expectations to be proud of my heritage.

My journey, struggle, and successes are all valid parts of my identity. I started to embrace my culture in my own way. Shame, embarrassment, and fear turned into pride, confidence, and courage. With this newfound voice, I confidently spoke up in meetings, shared ideas, and asserted opinions. Leveraging my diverse background and unique perspective, I brought invaluable strengths to the team. I became an advocate for diversity, equity, and inclusion (DEI), led cultural observance committees that recognized the historical achievements of Americans, and joined working groups whose purpose was to identify barriers related to equal opportunity and inclusion. Through these efforts, not only did I help others to find their voice, I found my sense of identity and purpose. I was no longer looking from the outside in; I put myself out there and integrated into places I once thought I didn't belong. I became part of a diverse community filled with support, mentorship, and lifelong friendships.

Through all this, I learned that I had to give myself grace. As I began to honor my heritage as a source of strength, I also had to be proud of my contributions. My insecurities burdened me for so long that I never felt comfortable celebrating my achievements because they didn't seem worthy. The reality was that my inability to speak Spanish or know the culture was so minute compared to all that I had gained and achieved. When all is said and done, I am doing what my grandparents dreamed of when they immigrated to this country. To provide a better life for children and grandchildren so that they can flourish and contribute positively to society. I've done that. I became a college graduate and blazed a successful, decorated military career. Achievements that would not have been possible without their sacrifices. I'm honoring their legacy. I have created a life that has made me proud to pay homage to all who have come before me. Motivated by pride, I became determined to be the best version of myself for my culture and those who come after me. I want to inspire the next generation of "no sabo" kids. They can know regardless of their inability to speak the language or lack of cultural knowledge, they are just as Hispanic as anyone else and have a place in this community.

Going through this journey, I've learned that there is no way to represent culture. It's about celebrating our differences, honoring our legacy, and forging our path. I don't have to fit the image of perceptions, and neither does anyone else who feels similarly marginalized. Finding my identity was about embracing what is authentically me, even with all the challenges that came with it. I use my voice to empower others and create a safe place for those who feel like they don't fit in. As I continue this journey of self-discovery, I stay committed to honoring those who have come before me by celebrating my culture, uplifting those around me, and breaking down barriers that go beyond stereotypes. I was free from shame, guilt, and inferiority by letting go of these expectations. I'm proud to be leaving a legacy that others can follow.

Being a "no sabo" kid is not a weakness but a source of strength. It's a tribute to the same resilience and power of persevering through adversity as our ancestors. You shouldn't be ashamed of being different or not fitting the mold. Your experiences, successes, and even failures are all part of what makes you who you are. It's this diversity that fuels the success of our culture. Finding your identity is not about how or where you can fit in; instead, it's about knowing that your experiences are valid, your contributions are valued, and you are leaving behind a proud legacy. As we move forward as a community, it's important that we remain united in supporting and celebrating all Hispanics, no matter how deep-rooted or not they are to the culture. We represent something larger than ourselves; we represent a legacy of unwavering resilience, hard work, and perseverance. We owe it to our ancestors and the future of Hispanic culture.

Josephine "Josie" Santana is a second-generation mixed Latina from Chicago. Early-life challenges led her to join the U.S. Air Force, where she is proudly serving over 20 years as a Senior Non-Commissioned Officer. She holds a bachelor's degree in human resources and is pursuing a graduate degree in Industrial/Organizational Psychology. She is a certified Department of the Air Force Leadership Coach. A dedicated advocate for Diversity, Equity, and Inclusion, Resiliency, and Violence Prevention, she has led over 100 cultural observances, professional seminars, and community events, effectively breaking down barriers and uniting diverse groups. Her innovative leadership has fostered resilience and equal opportunity. Josie's career is decorated with prestigious accolades, including the Military Outstanding Volunteer Service Medal and the Pacific Air Forces Command's 2020 nomination for the LATINA Style Distinguished Military Service Award and League of United Latin American Citizens award. Her journey exemplifies hard work, dedication, and perseverance.

Contact information for Josephine can be accessed here.

Saida Cornejo Zuñiga

Forjando Mi Camino: The Oldest Daughter of Immigrant Parents

My journey began in Michoacán, Mexico. *Mi tierra querida* that I left at the age of 6 months and have not returned. I don't remember my land yet feel so connected to it and to my *cultura*. It is a complicated feeling, being born in a place that I do not remember and yearning to return. While I do not remember my native land or the family I left behind, being born in La Mira, Michoacán, Mexico, has impacted every day of my life in the United States as an immigrant and the oldest daughter of immigrant parents.

My brave mother crossed the border and brought me to the United States when she was only 26 years old. There were many times when our lives were placed in danger, yet she had the courage to continue out of necessity and a fierce need to provide for her children. My parents sacrificed their lives for this country and never saw their parents again to afford their children a chance at an education and opportunity for a better life.

I had always liked school and can confidently confirm I was an overachiever, somewhat of a nerd in disguise. I started taking many AP classes and enrolled in local community college courses. When my counselor told me to apply for a STEM summer program, I did it. When my counselor highly encouraged me to apply for a college preparatory program at the University of California (UC) Berkeley, I did it. When I was required to apply to UC Berkeley by that same program, I did it without fully understanding the collegiate system and the influence that some universities hold.

In college, I learned the term for those higher achiever tendencies: hyper-documented. As a student, I held an ideology in my educational journey to be the best to compensate for something I could not change—my undocumented status. I tied my worthiness as a human being to my educational achievements. That perfectionism extended to every aspect of my life.

My journey was different. As an undocumented student, the odds were against me, and yet I was accepted to UC Berkeley. This was something I could not have achieved without the support of my parents. While they did not have the educational knowledge to guide me through the process, their encouragement and unwavering support in me made all the difference.

It was such an incredible moment for my family. A moment of pride for my parents and an example for my younger brothers. They, too, could one day attend an elite institution. At 5 years old, I was learning to speak English and had no idea what college was. My little brother, at the age of 5, was wearing Berkeley gear and professing he, too, was going to attend Berkeley.

2017 marked a transitional year for my family. I moved out to college and my dad launched his business. For 16 years, my dad was a painter, working for another company before bravely starting his own. In 2016, California passed a policy allowing undocumented individuals to apply for professional licenses. This allowed my dad to legitimize and open his own painting company. It also meant that as the oldest, it was expected of me to help my dad navigate this process.

While legal status was no longer a barrier, language and business knowledge continued to be. Not only was I a translator, but I also had to learn how to administer a business. It was my responsibility to learn about licensing, insurances, payroll, taxes, and more. While my peers at the time were worried about their courses and extracurricular activities, I was learning valuable skills without even realizing it—not because I wanted to, but because I had to. It's only now that I realize how much of my youth was spent handling responsibilities associated with adulthood.

Because of this sense of responsibility, I had never considered being so far away from home. However, that didn't limit me from pursuing my own career goals. After graduation, I applied to the Coro Fellows Program in Public Affairs, hoping to stay in the San Francisco Bay Area. When I was accepted to the program in St. Louis, I completely ignored the email. I could not fathom leaving my family and not being present when I was needed.

Oldest daughters in Latino households are expected to stay close to home. We are expected to learn to navigate the systems in the United States to help the family. Most of my life was spent supporting my dad in his small business, translating for my mom in healthcare settings, and guiding my brothers through the education system. I was the go-to person for any problem or issue that needed to be resolved. So, the mere thought of leaving my family, knowing they needed me, made me feel selfish and guilty. How dare I abandon my family to pursue something I wanted?

While my parents provided their unconditional support, it was hard for them to accept that their only daughter would be moving across the country. Although my mother never vocalized it, I knew me leaving was not what she wanted. What parent does? While he was extremely supportive of my need to get out of my comfort zone and grow, my dad knew I wouldn't be as available to support our business. We'd make it work.

I am proud that I took this leap to forge my own path outside of the family nucleus because St. Louis is where I came into my power and voice. Throughout my life, I had always had to be the voice of the family but had never done so for myself. I was thrown out of my comfort zone when I moved across the country at 23 years old. It pushed me to navigate the unknown and advocate for myself.

St. Louis is where I learned to be comfortable in my own skin. It's where I came to terms with being the only Latina in the room and not feeling uncomfortable by it. St. Louis is where I learned to activate my power and use my voice.

While I was experiencing this new journey, the feelings of responsibility to my family did not magically disappear. Not only was there a sense of responsibility but also of guilt for not being present and readily available. I wasn't supporting my dad with the small business as often as I had been. I worried that my mother wasn't receiving comprehensive healthcare because of a language barrier. I was no longer experiencing my brothers' educational milestones firsthand. And while my parents were not resentful of me for taking this opportunity, it is hard to distance myself from this pressure that has been ingrained in me from a young age.

This newfound power that I embraced wasn't just for my benefit, it extended to my whole family. Earlier this year, I traveled to California to visit my mom, who had been having health issues. That same week, my dad had a misunderstanding with one of his clients at a job site. Due to the language barrier, it was difficult for my dad to understand her and vice versa. She was rude and degrading to someone she looked down on—someone with darker skin and *mestizo* features, a complexion I have proudly inherited from my parents. I was not going to allow someone to treat my family that way. If she wanted to speak to someone who spoke English fluently, then she'd direct herself to me.

I accompanied my dad to the job site, and with a firm handshake, I introduced myself and expressed my desire to clear up any confusion. The power that I felt in standing up for myself and for my family was a result of me forging my own path. I have learned to channel the anger and fear that comes with standing up for yourself and to do it regardless. Two years ago, I would have never had the courage to confront this client.

Oldest daughters lead the family nucleus, but that does not mean we cannot have our own story. I have led and continue to lead my family. However, I have also learned to listen to that part of me that craves independence and the space to focus on my own career and aspirations. While beautiful, it is not always a smooth journey, and that's okay. I am still in the process of unlearning the patterns of dependency that I have enabled and embracing the emotions that come with it. The biggest lesson I've learned is that when I'm good, my family is good. At this place in my journey, I look back grateful to God and for my family's support and look forward to a bright future as I independently build a new path.

Saida Cornejo Zuñiga was born in Michoacán, Mexico, and raised in the Bay Area, California. She attended the University of California, Berkeley, where she majored in Ethnic Studies and Legal Studies, further igniting her passion for immigrant entrepreneurship.

She came to St. Louis as a Coro Fellow in Public Affairs, a cross-sector civic leadership development program that broadened her understanding of the region. Her growing appreciation for the city led her to join Alderwoman Daniela Velázquez's team as the 6th Ward Legislative Aide for the City of St. Louis, where she spearheaded ward initiatives and conducted policy analysis.

Dedicated to uplifting the Latino community, Saida also joined the Board of the Hispanic Leaders Group of Greater St. Louis as the Legislative Affairs Committee Chair. Currently, Saida is the Recruitment and Capital Access Lead at WEPOWER, where she guides Black and Latinx entrepreneurs through small business accelerators and funding opportunities.

Ninfa Mayta

Quizá Nunca Calladita
Las Voces de Mi Niñez

I would get in trouble again and again in kindergarten for constantly talking and making people laugh at nap time in a school in the Rio Grande Valley. I was very confused about what was so bad about talking, especially if it made my classmates laugh. Some of them slept. How could they sleep?

There were strong cultural and faith-based voices that I heard as a child migrating through Texas, Michigan, Washington, Ohio, Indiana, Arkansas, Missouri, and Illinois. I remember listening to my aunts and uncles fighting for *la causa*. "Chicano Power!" my *Tia* Lali and *Tio* Lupe would march for Hispanic rights. Some people ignored Chicano voices, while others jailed them. Some people, like me, were inspired by them. As kids, we three made picket signs and echoed the words, "Chicano Power! Chicano Power!" That was our game. We just kept repeating it and marching in a circle. My older brother, Leroy, led us, and it was exhilaratingly convicting. He still has that effect on us today. I can't remember the year we stopped doing this. We had many moves, many life changes as Texan American migrants, constantly yanked by crop harvests.

I also heard voices say, *"Usted, Mami"* as my parents, aunts, uncles, and cousins addressed my grandparents. The language around my elders required me to use respectful words when addressing others, especially during religious matters. They were extra cautious with me since they believed an outspoken person would tend to be outspoken wherever they are, or as they say in Spanish—*Un buen gallo, dondequiera canta.* Or...

¡Cállate, por favor! I heard this often on our migrating family road trips. Upon one migration move, my mom put my vocal strengths to the test and ordered me to sit in the front seat, in her full frustration with my voice. "Now, don't let your dad fall asleep on the trip!" With a pouting start, I shrugged quickly and learned that I could talk about anything for about 30 hours. I asked my dad about everything as he chuckled. "Pop, who paints the lines on the highway, and who installs the reflective signs?" All the while, my three siblings, Leroy, Luciano, and Baby Araceli, always seemed to be asleep. How could they sleep? I always woke everyone up anytime we crossed the Mississippi.

We were on the road a great deal as we lived and migrated in the agricultural ways, means, and *campos* until I was 7 years old. Once we settled in Holland, Michigan, I kept my *cotorra* co-pilot legacy as a tradition while my dad would take us back to Texas to visit during a glorious Christmas time to be with extended family in the "Valley." My dad drove straight through, which meant no sleep from Michigan to the tip of palm-filled Southern Texas. I was the "Audible" for 30 hours, while the song that played over and over on the radio was "I Wanna Wish you a Merry Christmas" by Jose Feliciano, and, of course, Tejano music once we hit the Texas state line.

It was while living permanently in Michigan that I received my formal education. Being outspoken continued to plague me and my parents. It was difficult for me during my teenage life as I always wanted to join social events, meet cute boys, and join school programs. My song was "Girls Just

Want to Have Fun." I felt trapped, and I began to exaggerate my suffering pangs of oppression and depression at being kept at bay.

Las Voces de Crecer Como Adulto

While studying at Western Michigan University, I engaged in student organizations. As the president of the Hispanic Student Organization, I was instrumental in bringing motivational speakers such as Cesar Chavez, Jaime Escalante, and several others. I did not have a fear of speaking. In fact, I found that I needed to curb my over-lively way of speaking. I coveted the power and poise of quiet people like my sister, Araceli.

While I was studying, I signed up for exuberant speaking and singing assignments during our semester breaks. I was part of a troupe that proclaimed messages directed to recruit high school students, hoping to influence them to stay in school and to "Just Say No" to sex and drugs. I wished for them a life of choices. From this, I was also appointed to serve as the representative voice for Hispanics for the university president. What a different experience I had compared to my aunts' and uncles' generation, who experienced "stolen education!" The racial, cultural, and economic inequalities were still present; however, they were painfully subtle.

After graduating and attending several Chicago Hispanic Leadership Conferences, I was inspired to help my brother get elected to the City Council. I loved campaigning for Luciano because he was so well-trained and respected. He, like my grandfather, was a great spokesperson and role model for our community. I was so proud to work for and encourage our Hispanic and non-Hispanic community to vote. Ours seemed to be a dormant community without a voice but a community that was and is chock-full of dreams. Luciano won! We won with our motto, "*Su Voto es Su Voz*."

What was next for my life was working in my field and serving on boards where my voice was welcome. It was an opportunity to make a difference. During one of our moves, I found these words in a journal—

"I yearn to be on a board." This came years after I had served on a chemical board out of college, as an advisor to the university president, on a Catholic school board, on an art museum board, and on pastoral counsel to name a few.

Throughout my vocation, I continued seeking to hone my message, my voice, for others. I joined professional organizations like Toastmasters International and Dale Carnegie. Many people wondered why I was there since most other people were there to come out of their shells. However, I realized that they could help me channel my voice, channel my strengths to make a difference in my relationships, and in my fueled, projectized life. The most valuable lesson I learned was that voiceless and shy people will break out of their silence with the right channeled encouragement toward their purpose and expertise. I witnessed this painful metamorphosis in them, which in turn, changed my perspective.

Shaping my voice for other people—now that's intentionality. It was with the Maxwell Leadership Team that I was fortunate enough to go to Paraguay and Costa Rica, where I coached and impacted other coaches to reach a new level of their potential. Because I was a bilingual chatterbox, I was offered to go into *provincia* to reach the remote voiceless. There were people speaking out for their futures like they never had. Their governments knew that their people needed inspiration to grow, yet it was I who grew. I cried with them, and I am so grateful for our team of 200 coaches. We ended up reaching and speaking to over 15,000 people in each of these countries.

I continue to coach others, as I love extracting their dreams and seeing their goals come to fruition. I remember one who wanted to change his job, and I asked what he worked in. He painted lines for the highway. I finally knew where the lines came from on a personal basis. Things seemed to come to fulfillment after decades.

My rewarding experience as a coach to the voiceless leads me to professional, tireless single moms or selfless working dads being heads of their households. I've helped several of them as immigrants find their inner strength to go back to visit their countries and find that family member or mentor they longed to see in Bolivia, Laos, and Nigeria.

Mi Voz para Mis Próximos Pasos

I dedicate my chapter to my Aunt Lali Saenz Moheno and her husband, *Tio* Victor B. Moheno. They helped shape my voice, my talents, and my vision. What an understatement of love!

I will see them soon, and my non-*callada* voice will let them know I am grateful for their love and efforts. I highly laud my *Tia* as she is the voice for the voiceless Women Farm Workers in California. She and her team give back tirelessly, so I must, and I am destined as well. That summarizes me and the work I still need to voice and do. *Primero Dios.*

I use my silent prayer voice to invoke the Holy Spirit so that I may not grow tired and may work for others. I use my voice to invoke Jesus' love in the way I treat others. And I voice my call to God for powerful courage to see the path, know the path, and go the path He has planned for me.

Ninfa Mayta received a bachelor's degree of Science in Engineering Graphics from Kalamazoo, Michigan. She also holds a master of science in Management. This placed a focus on project management in Colorado Springs, Colorado. Through the Project Management Institute, she is a certified Project Management Professional (PMP) and Portfolio Management Professional (PfMP) with certifications earned in Minneapolis, Minnesota, and St. Louis, Missouri.

Ninfa is also a Distinguished Toastmaster (DTM) through Toastmasters International in Minneapolis, Minnesota. Based in Orlando, Florida, she is a certified coach, trainer, and speaker with the Maxwell Leadership Certified Team. Her extensive educational background and professional certifications highlight her commitment to leadership and project management excellence.

Contact information for Ninfa can be accessed here.

Alexandra Johnson

Joy and Authenticity Are Your North Star

Heal yourself;

get rid of anything that doesn't help heal you;

cultivate your joy.

~Alexandra Johnson

"I'm a boy!" At a young age of about 4, I realized that boys got to do things girls did not. I declared myself a boy. There! Problem solved! I'm a boy now, so I can do whatever I want. I've been fighting sexism and other battles ever since I realized a simple announcement by me wasn't going to change the world.

I am a proud *mestiza*—part Mexican, part *güera*, part atheist, part Roman Catholic, part repressed, part sexually free, part abused, part healed. I am undeniably privileged, but my years on this earth so far have also been marked with any number of adverse events. I have used the blows as well as the blessings to forge a life that is rewarding and joyful on many levels.

Looking back, I have always been the hero of my own story and saved myself, *desde chiquita*. Truthfully, I don't know how I had the inner strength to do so. From childhood on, I pushed back at predators and ended toxic connections. I invested in myself and eventually found a safe partner with whom to raise a family.

Recently, I kept myself safe again—because I'm worth it. A man groped me. It was a light touch, a rubbing of my bra and underarm area as we were casually hugging goodbye, quite common in Hispanic culture. His subtle, quick gesture was to see if I was interested. Just as subtly, and with grace, full of composure, and aplomb, I discreetly pressed his hand away from my body. We barely made eye contact as he left.

I was really upset, both in that moment and because it was a trigger of past ordeals. Nevertheless, as usual, I had to find a way to move forward despite this struggle. I called on strength gleaned from overcoming past challenges. I stuck to my new fitness routine. I checked in with my husband and a couple of friends whose opinions I trust. I stunned myself by not feeling shame, which would have been my go-to response based on past wounds, my deeply conservative religious upbringing, and even my cultural heritage regarding my femininity and sexuality.

Some lessons were gleaned from this event, but I did not—and do not now—take ownership of that man's misdeed. I am completely clear in my mind that it was not my fault. In fact, *no harm **ever** done to me was my fault.*

As I processed this experience, the reminder of men's power in our society overall and of my past sexual assaults was hurtful and scary, but the goddess part of me took over. I allowed myself to move through my feelings as wholesomely as possible. I proved to myself that I would show up for me.

In my process of becoming the butterfly that I am, I have been shedding my caterpillar ways. I am ridding myself of whatever parts of my family's emotional legacy don't serve me anymore. I'm replacing coping methods I often had no choice but to adopt with focused, intentional, and effective self-care.

With this latest violation, I tended to my needs softly and lovingly, transmuting the suffering into nourishment of my core strength. What am I tapping into as I realize my full potential as a human being? How have I always been a *luchadorsita* from the beginning? I credit the immigrant grit inherited from those who came before me because I am a pioneer from a land of dysfunction into a healthier, more positive headspace.

Much of my trauma occurred within the family, so culling the wheat from the chaff was essential. I found courage from my Swedish grandfather, who, as one cousin tells it, turned at the end of the dirt road to look back at his parents one last time before coming to the United States to avoid starvation. He knew he would likely never see them and his country again, but he embarked on his journey anyway. From my German grandmother, who ceaselessly toiled on a Minnesota farm to build a life for the family, I inherited perseverance. *Mi Mamita Chula* was a fierce, imperfect, loving, brilliant, courageous woman who, though from a wealthy family, came to the United States to pursue an innovative career in academics. My dad was a strict but, in many ways, loving father and servant of God. Together, they showed me how to live according to one's principles.

I can't forget *mi Abuelita Chula*! She was not a *Luchadora*, but she was a fierce survivor until her last days. What I have been told is that she was orphaned as a child during the Mexican Revolution. Later, she lived in a convent as a servant when *mi Abuelito*, a self-made man and widower, met her when he was making deliveries. Before refrigeration, folks ordered ice and potable water brought to them, and one of her duties to earn her keep was to open the convent gate (*el portón*).

The fruits of my grandfather's labor were not insignificant. *La casa de mis abuelitos* had many bedrooms, multiple bathrooms, stained glass windows in the dining room, tiles specially imported from Portugal decorating some of the walls, a swimming pool, an orchard, a tennis court, and more. My grandmother, in turn, bore him several children while also raising the children from his deceased first wife, for a total of 13 kids and *lots* of grandchildren.

Their resilience and enterprising spirit fully infuse my independent mindset to this day. The immigrant, go-getter spirit of my elders never allowed me to quit anything of significance. Even when I was studying for the bar exam with actual tears rolling down my cheeks because I was so mentally exhausted, I kept going. When family has not been supportive, I have kept going. Despite getting sore from trying to get in shape, I have kept going. When unresolved pain made me afraid to explore myself, my sexuality, and my most suppressed emotions, *I have kept going.*

My north star in my quest to thrive, not just survive, is composed of these new guiding principles:

1. Heal myself. No one can force me to take care of myself. That must come from within.

2. Jettison what is no longer helping me mend myself, such as old coping mechanisms, clutter, and unhelpful relationships of any kind.

3. Prioritize *joy!* By nurturing my authenticity, assembling my own village of genuine allies, and grounding myself in gratitude, I have overcome my fears. If I'm still scared, I do it anyway!

In this liminal phase that I am in—this transformation into a *mariposa* and learning how to spread my wings and fly—I'm letting go of the me that is comfortable and familiar to become the me I've always wanted to be. I've had to unearth parts of myself that were covered in trauma, like the layers of an archeological dig into my soul. It has been and continues to be such arduous work!

As I catch glimpses of my new self, my personal and professional accomplishments are proof evident of my tenacity. They show me I can overcome a great deal. I studied law and international business simultaneously, completing the separate programs in four years instead of five. I speak German, French, and Spanish. I have often pursued my goals with no precedent. An example is that, to my knowledge, I was the first Latina to run for citywide office in St. Louis and the first Hispanic to run for citywide office in decades (St. Louis did have a Hispanic mayor, Alfonso Cervantes, but that was in 1965-1973). My marriage is healthy enough for us to heal and delve into our sexuality together. My volunteering has been kindly acknowledged in many ways, including with peer-based awards for my work in the community.

My take? Don't be afraid to be the first at anything—create your own path. Don't allow fear to stop you. Know that any harm done to any of us was **not** our fault! It's not possible to get back to the original version of us, the *tabula rasa* we were at birth, so don't waste your precious minutes in the attempt.

My suggestion is to focus on discovering, accepting, and honoring the beauty of who you truly are now—embrace *kintsugi*, the Japanese art of beautifully and visibly repairing broken items. Your scars are reminders of having survived your worst day. Don't come to the end of your time without having given yourself the boon of loving yourself fully and unconditionally and unapologetically.

Heal yourself. Get rid of what doesn't serve you. Like the monarch *mariposa* on its way up and down to Mexico, use *the joy of your own authenticity* as your north star. Dear reader, telling you my story has comforted me. Hopefully, my road map benefits you as well. *¡Buena suerte! ¡Te deseo lo mejor!*

La Luchadorsita: Alexandra Johnson is an estate planning attorney in private practice in St. Louis, Missouri. From her earliest awareness as a child, Alex fought to protect herself from trauma as best she could—as she does to this day. She has overcome life's many challenges by drawing on the strength of her ancestors and a fierce, if sometimes unconscious, self-love. She habitually prioritizes her loved ones, clients, and volunteering, but this time, she's stepping up for herself. In writing for the *Calladitas Rising* anthology, she revamps her internal compass, creating a new frame of reference for her own self-worth, one apart from her upbringing and one that recognizes herself as the hero of her own story. Alex stands in her own power as she shares her road map for healing in the hopes of lifting others up as she rises to her full potential as a human being.

Dórothy Guillén

Embracing My Voice

Growing up in Colombia, cultural expectations were clear: women were to be submissive, obedient, and quiet. These norms influenced every aspect of my identity and choices. I knew that I needed to break free from these expectations to truly thrive. *Calladita te ves más bonita* was a phrase frequently directed at me, constantly reminding me that my worth was tied to being quiet and compliant.

The Call to Challenge

My journey began when I pursued an associate degree in mechanical engineering. In a field dominated by men, my presence was often questioned, and my capabilities underestimated. I vividly remember moments of doubt and condescension from my peers and instructors. Despite the fear and potential consequences, I felt compelled to speak up. I knew that my voice and perspective were valuable, even if those around me couldn't see it yet.

One pivotal moment came during a particularly challenging project in my mechanical engineering program. Despite my contributions and hard work, my male colleagues sought to sideline me, assuming I couldn't handle the technical aspects and relegating me to peripheral tasks. I faced overt sexism and discrimination, with my abilities constantly questioned.

Navigating with *Malicia Indígena*

Throughout my journey, I often relied on what Colombians call *malicia indígena*. This term refers to an innate cunning or shrewdness that enables one to find solutions and overcome issues creatively. *Malicia indígena* is a form of street smarts deeply rooted in our indigenous heritage that combines intuition with practical wisdom. It is an ability to navigate complex situations with a keen sense of awareness and adaptability.

The challenges I faced in mechanical engineering were not unique to me. Many women in male-dominated fields experience similar obstacles, however, I learned to use *malicia indígena* to my advantage. I observed how my male colleagues interacted and learned to anticipate their moves. I found ways to prove my competence subtly, ensuring that my contributions were undeniable. This strategy helped me survive in a hostile environment, but it also made me realize that I needed to find a place where I could truly thrive, not just survive.

A New Path

Despite my successes, the pervasive gender bias in mechanical engineering was suffocating. I realized that to fully utilize my talents and passion, I needed to pivot to a different career. This decision was not easy. It felt like admitting defeat, but I reframed it as a strategic move to find a field where my voice could flourish.

I decided to pursue a career in finance and accounting, a field that still had its challenges but offered more opportunities for growth and recognition. My technical knowledge and accounting skills gave me the opportunity to succeed in several companies, demonstrating my abilities to shine and oversee multiple projects managed by men to make decisions that were beneficial to the company.

As part of my destiny, I fell in love with an American man and moved to the United States 10 years ago with minimal English knowledge. The story repeated itself as I grappled with self-doubt and fear. The constant message that women should be seen and not heard, deeply ingrained in my psyche, flourished again.

In addition to gender-based challenges, being an immigrant added another layer of complexity. Moving to the United States for better opportunities, I faced cultural and language barriers. My accent and background often made me the target of prejudice. These experiences only fueled my determination.

Pursuing Excellence

I enrolled in an MBA program at Webster University in Missouri, driven by the desire to equip myself with the skills and knowledge needed to excel. First, however, I needed to complete an extensive English as a Second Language (ESL) program. It really challenged me not only to read, write, and speak in a completely new way but also to understand the global perspectives of a plethora of other students from Asia, Europe, North America, and South America.

I became engrossed in studying with and learning from my new friends. Additionally, I was able to travel internationally with my husband, whose profession took him literally around the globe on a regular basis. I was able to tie the descriptions my classmates provided about their cultures, foods, dances, and landscapes back to the stories of their homelands. I truly felt at home visiting foreign lands and developing a greater understanding and knowledge of new things. I felt at ease in the world it seemed.

Nonetheless, the transition to the United States was fraught with challenges. I was still an immigrant in a foreign country, navigating a new cultural landscape while dealing with the complexities of a rigorous academic program. Despite these hurdles, I remained resolute in proving that my voice, shaped by a diverse cultural background, held power and worth. I was determined to continue my career growth and gain the same respect I already earned in the Latin American market.

As I progressed through the MBA program, I began to see myself in a new light. My confidence grew, bolstered by academic achievements and the support of my husband, my family, my mentors, and my peers. I realized that my identity was not defined by societal expectations but by my own choices and actions. I began to advocate for myself and others, using my voice to highlight issues of gender inequality and to support my fellow students.

Building Bread and Bake LLC

Despite my professional success, I felt a longing to connect more deeply with my cultural roots and to create something that was entirely my own. This led to the birth of Bread and Bake LLC. I left my position as an executive-level international accounting professional and channeled my passion into creating a bakery that combined my Colombian heritage with artisan baking. The decision was both thrilling and terrifying. I was leaving a secure career to venture into the unknown, but I believed in my vision.

One of the most rewarding aspects of starting Bread and Bake LLC was the opportunity to build a community. I used my voice to connect with customers, sharing the stories behind my products and the cultural significance of my recipes. I also collaborated with other local businesses and participated in community events, using these platforms to advocate for cultural diversity and female empowerment.

I would like to continue mentoring young women, providing internships and job opportunities at my bakery. I want to create a supportive environment where women can thrive and develop their skills. By sharing my journey and the lessons I learned along the way, I hope to inspire the next generation of female entrepreneurs.

The Power of My Voice

Using my voice has had a profound impact on my life and the lives of those around me. It has allowed me to break free from the constraints of cultural and gender expectations, to build a successful career in a male-dominated field, earning the right to be a subject matter expert in international accounting and finance, and to create a business that celebrates my heritage. My journey has been one of resilience and personal development, marked by the constant challenge to assert myself and advocate for change.

As I look to the future, I am committed to continuing this journey of empowerment. I plan to expand Bread and Bake LLC, reaching more customers and creating opportunities for women. I will continue to use my voice to advocate for change, challenge prejudices, and inspire others to speak up.

My story is just one of many in the *Calladitas Rising* anthology, but it proves the power of finding and using one's voice. It is a reminder that silence is not a virtue and that our voices are our greatest tools for change. By sharing our stories, we can inspire others, build a supportive community, and create a more just and equitable world.

Finding and using my voice has been a journey of resilience, empowerment, and growth. It has required me to overcome internal and external barriers, to break free from cultural expectations, and to rely on my innate skills, such as *malicia indígena*. My voice has become a powerful tool, not just for myself but for others who face similar challenges.

As I continue on this path, I am reminded that every step I take is a step toward greater equality and empowerment. My voice, once silenced by cultural norms and gender expectations, is now a beacon of hope and change. I am proud of my journey, and I look forward to the future with optimism and determination.

Born on April 14, 1975, in Bogotá, Colombia, Dórothy was raised in a disadvantaged neighborhood where only 1 percent of residents had access to higher education. Thanks to her mother's relentless efforts, she and her two siblings achieved their goal to be educated. Holding an associate degree in mechanical engineering, then pivoting to the accounting field, Dórothy moved to the United States a decade ago, pursuing an MBA and overcoming language barriers to advance her career. With the steadfast support of her husband, she founded Bread and Bake, channeling her passion for artisan baking into a successful business.

Contact information for Dórothy can be accessed here.

Juliana Castellanos-Heath

Finding Strength in Vulnerability

Growing up, I was encouraged to speak up and treat everyone equally. My parents raised me to be an independent, professional woman. My mom's influence was evident in my actions every day. She led by example, always speaking the truth. My dad taught me the importance of thoughtful communication and using education to debate effectively. However, they didn't prepare me for the societal challenges I would face as a woman like me, often silenced by others.

I'm from Facatativá, a town near Bogotá, Colombia, which means "strong fence at the end of the plain" in the indigenous Muisca language. Growing up in a small town in a traditionally *machista* culture with traditional values and being the only woman among my three siblings gave me a mix of old-fashioned values and feminism. Most of my family remains in Facatativá except for my older brother, who lives in New Jersey. This is why I initially came to the United States.

My parents instilled the values of helping others and serving the community. They often went beyond their limits for others. One day, while walking back home in *el parque de las Tinguas*, I remember my dad saying that the purpose of life was to be happy. To achieve that, you need to create or provide value to society. This statement became my mission, though it seemed a distant dream for a long time due to life's challenges.

I practiced gymnastics from ages 9 to 13. With my family deeply involved in the sport, my parents as coaches, and my brothers as gymnasts, training sessions were like family time. When I decided to quit, I lost that family time, and at 13 years old, that was confusing. Unfortunately, I started experimenting with drugs and alcohol, leading to a decade-long struggle with addiction. During my teenage years, I caused immense pain to my family and experienced microtraumas myself.

Addiction has been a hard label to carry, making me an outlier in society for a long time. I ended up in a five-year abusive and toxic relationship that was *la última gota que derramó el vaso*. I lost myself, I lost my voice, and I almost lost my family. I was one of those people whom families and friends at some point wanted to give up on, one of those whom *chismosos* would say wasn't worth supporting anymore, which is why I'm so grateful to those who didn't give up on me.

Life continued to challenge me, and it was hard to maintain the belief that "life knows what it's doing." Balancing addiction with medical school was difficult. Though I excelled intellectually, addiction hindered my focus and performance. Toward the end of my medical career, I faced severe bullying after rejecting a chief resident's sexual advances. He used his authority to enable others to mistreat me, and when I spoke up, it only worsened my situation. Despite raising concerns, I endured three months of repercussions for "accusing" the residents.

I kept the true nature of the problem hidden, even from my mother. It wasn't until this year, during one of our healing conversations, that I finally revealed the real cause of the bullying. When she asked why I hadn't spoken out earlier, I explained that my voice wouldn't be taken seriously due to my struggles with addiction. I chose silence because I was certain that no one would believe me over him.

Each challenge was a raw cut, but like the skin, I've grown back, wiser and more resilient, though a little less innocent. I completed medical school, became a doctor, and got sober in 2015. After three years of sobriety, I decided to quit my job as a general practitioner in November 2019 and travel across Central and South America. My goal was to join Doctors Without Borders and continue traveling with them.

I decided to come to the United States to practice English and improve my chances of being accepted into an international healthcare nonprofit. I arrived in New York on February 6, just days before the global health emergency was declared. The pandemic thwarted my plans—Colombia closed its borders, preventing my return, and Doctors Without Borders rejected my application. I was naive and thought my plan would go smoothly but little did I know that life is surprisingly difficult.

Stuck in the United States, I luckily had my brother in New Jersey, who offered support and a couch to crash on for three months. I tried to stay optimistic, believing there was no crisis I couldn't handle. My savings quickly ran out. I needed to take action. I found a job as a waitress in a Colombian restaurant in New Jersey. Though it kept me afloat, it didn't help my English and it was hitting my ego, even if I didn't want to accept it at the time.

I was struggling with uncertainty about my future. Plan A, traveling across North, South, and Central America, was canceled due to the pandemic. Plan B, applying to Doctors Without Borders, was also canceled. Plan C, returning home, was impossible because of the pandemic-related border closures. I felt lost and unsure of my next steps. I decided to pursue a medical license in the United States as a survival strategy, knowing it was one of the hardest and longest processes. My optimistic self believed that if others could do it, so could I.

While working as a waitress and studying, my friend from St. Louis, whom I had briefly dated back in the day when he lived in Colombia, invited me to visit in the summer of 2020. I went, not knowing much about Missouri. By the end of the week together, he invited me back for his birthday a month later. I returned to St. Louis with a one-way ticket. Today, I've been married to my friend, my lover, and my main supporter for almost three years, and I am grateful for this unexpected turn in my life. Staying in this country for love was the craziest, most courageous, and adventurous decision I've ever made.

Immigration has reshaped my identity, adding the challenges of adapting as a minority and my new phase as a wife. I spiraled but was determined not to fail. I pushed through, stepping out of my comfort zone and trying to find a way to use my profession in the United States. Without a license, my options were limited to temporary, non-medical jobs. My options were research, secretarial work in healthcare, a waitress, or a cleaner. They were dignified jobs I did temporarily, but not what I had envisioned for my future.

With support and time, I connected with other immigrants, particularly women, who were building new lives. This changed everything. I networked and aimed for a public health job I had dreamed of. My husband taught me to drive, helping me gain independence and confidence. I even turned down jobs that weren't right for me because I knew I could contribute more to this community.

My first healthcare job in the United States came through resilience and determination. I spoke to many people, volunteered, and did over 30 informational interviews. I finally secured my current position directing an HIV/STI prevention program, allowing me to work for those in need.

Adapting to the workforce has meant confronting cultural clashes and navigating new labels. One of the most challenging experiences has been being labeled "aggressive" simply for expressing my opinions or disagreeing. It's been difficult to connect with others when I'm often seen through the lens of what makes me different—my skin color, accent, or appearance. Recently, referring to my accent as "cute" or "sexy" in professional contexts has been particularly frustrating, complicating my efforts to build deep and meaningful relationships.

The label of "immigrant" came with its own baggage, and for months, I struggled to manage it. Talking to other immigrants, particularly Hispanic women, helped me understand that the problem wasn't me but cultural differences and people's reluctance to understand them. Over time, I've been accepting many of these labels as part of my reality and new identity. I've come to understand their role in my life, and ultimately embracing them has made me stronger.

Lately, I feel I'm getting closer to achieving my mission of finding happiness and contributing to society. I know I will continue to face challenges and adversity—especially as an immigrant, woman, and strong individual—where forces will always try to silence me.

I've learned the key: believe in myself and embrace change. I no longer resist. I now ask myself, "What is life trying to teach me through these challenges?" Life can be chaotic and demands great resilience. There will be moments of tears and struggle. Be courageous and compassionate with yourself. Speak up, and don't let others or circumstances bring you down. Find the people who will support and uplift you, including a good therapist. That's the formula I've applied to become a fearless woman.

Juliana Castellanos is a passionate individual from Colombia with a caring nature, embracing vulnerability as her superpower to connect deeply with others and offer meaningful support. She has faced challenges multiple times, and her ability to bounce back has become a guiding force in her life. Juliana left her country to embark on an adventurous journey, which was unexpectedly halted by a pandemic that kept her in the United States longer than expected. She has been living in St. Louis, Missouri, for four years, where she has integrated into the community to serve it. Her passion and determination in her career as a physician, currently working in public health directing an STI prevention program, have allowed her to pour her heart into helping those in need. Her strong inclination to overthink and over feel life continues to shape her journey.

Contact information for Juliana can be accessed here.

Leonor Branch

Resilience, Courage, and the Power of Finding Your Voice

My journey began not with grand ambitions but with a deep, personal challenge—a quest to break through cultural and personal barriers. As a Latina woman joining the military, I set out to serve my country and discover my own strength. Little did I know that this path would lead me to embrace leadership and empowerment in ways I never imagined. My story is a reflection of resilience, courage, and the power of finding one's voice.

Facing Family Expectations

The decision to join the military was met with skepticism from my family and community. In our culture, traditional roles for women are often seen as the norm. Pursuing a career in the military seemed almost rebellious. I felt torn between my desire to serve and my responsibilities at home. *Mi querida mamá*, who relied on me for support due to language barriers, was particularly concerned. Leaving her behind was heart-wrenching, but I knew my youngest sister would step up to help her. The weight of this decision was heavy, yet I was driven by a vision of breaking free from expectations and charting a new course. I also knew that *mi mamá's rezos* (prayers) to *la Virgen Maria Santisima* would protect me. Now as a mother of three, I can't imagine what she went through when her *cookita* left for good. Her prayers guided me through the hardest times when I felt alone and sometimes defeated.

My parents and family immigrated to the United States for work, family, and school. My mom, at the age of 19, was the oldest of the siblings, struggled with the new culture but was ready to put their hands to work like they did growing up in Mexico. It was a risky move to leave as a family of eight—*mi mamá, mi papá, tías, tíos y abuelitos*. As they struggled through poverty and finding their place in life, my parents were hit with a surprise soon after their arrival. They were expecting their first child. My parents, not knowing how they would afford bringing up a new baby in the world, put their trust in God to guide them through.

Overcoming Language Barriers

Joining the military as a non-native English speaker added another layer of difficulty. Effective communication was crucial for my success, so I dedicated myself to improving my language skills. My first significant test came during basic training at Lackland Air Force Base, Texas. I was assigned as the chow runner, a role that required me to navigate the intimidating "snake pit" of male drill instructors. When they demanded I recite my reporting statement in Spanish, I took a deep breath and delivered it with pride, "*Señor entrenador Roman se reporta como ordenado vuelo 634 está preparado para entrar el lado oeste.*" Their laughter in response to my defiance was a mix of mockery and surprise, but I used that moment as fuel. Standing tall and speaking my native language in a space that seemed so foreign was a declaration of my resolve.

The Pivotal Moment

One of the most transformative moments in my life occurred during my service when I experienced a few seizures. This health crisis forced me to confront not only my physical limitations but also my emotional resilience. At a time when I was transitioning into a new role as a recruiter, I faced severe challenges. My ability to drive was compromised, and the neurological issues from the seizure made everyday tasks difficult. How could I lead and inspire others when I was grappling with my own struggles?

Drawing inspiration from my family's resilience, who had worked tirelessly in Mexico and in the United States to provide a better life for my cousins and me, I persevered. I thought of the late nights *mi mamá* came home from working all day to take care of her *hermanos* and my sister and me. I watched her push through moments of exhaustion but never let herself be defeated. Despite the odds, I immersed myself in my new role. I attended high school visits, career fairs, and late-night admin work. My determination paid off when I was awarded Blue Suit—a program that selects the best from nearly 1,600 Air Force recruiters worldwide and top recruiter in the nation. This recognition was more than just a professional achievement; it was a profound affirmation of my capabilities and evidence of my journey through adversity. A moment I could not have gone through without the help of *mi familia*.

Embracing Leadership and Empowerment

The challenges I faced during my military career fueled my passion for preventative care and health awareness. The Latino community is disproportionately affected by various medical conditions, and I realized the critical importance of fitness and health education. My role as a fitness coach allowed me to advocate for wellness and inspire others to prioritize their health.

Creating Sisters in Service (SIS) – Greater St. Louis was a natural extension of my journey post-military. This nonprofit organization is dedicated to supporting women veterans as they transition out of military life. SIS provides resources, support, and a sense of community for women who have served. It's a platform where we share our stories, find strength in one another, and empower each other to thrive. A beacon of hope so that no woman is left behind.

A Return to My Roots

My experiences led me to a powerful moment of reflection and reconnection with my roots. After years of service and being restricted from visiting Mexico Taxco, Guerrero, I finally returned to my homeland 24 years later. The trip was a journey back to my origins—dancing in el Zócalo to Selena's "Queen of Tejano Music" and revisiting childhood memories walking through *el mercado* and eating *pan dulce*. This return was a reminder of the cultural richness and familial bonds that shaped me. It was a liberating experience that reaffirmed my identity and embraced my heritage.

My journey from a young Latina facing cultural barriers to becoming a leader in the nonprofit and fitness industries is evidence of the power of perseverance and self-belief. My story serves as a reminder that breaking down barriers and overcoming adversity is possible. Embrace your voice, trust in your abilities, and let your journey inspire others. Finding your voice and breaking free from limitations is not just about personal success; it's about creating a ripple effect that empowers others to follow suit. My story is an invitation to all women—especially those from underrepresented backgrounds—to embrace their leadership potential and make their mark on the world.

As a Latina woman in the military, finding my voice and maintaining my cultural identity has been a journey filled with challenges. One pivotal moment that stands out occurred during my last few years of service. I was in the office, speaking Spanish with a fellow Latino colleague. For a moment, it felt like a piece of home had found its way into the rigid structure of military life. However, I noticed that our conversation seemed to make our peers uncomfortable.

Curious and wanting to address the tension, I asked if they found it rude. One of my coworkers confirmed my suspicion, saying yes. In that moment, I felt a wave of conformity wash over me. Despite the significance of speaking my native language, I turned to my colleague and asked him to stop speaking Spanish. It felt like a betrayal of my roots, but at the time, it seemed necessary to fit in. Years of service had distanced me from my cultural heritage, and I had even begun to lose fluency in Spanish. The brief connection I had with my colleague was a rare opportunity to reclaim a part of my identity, but I silenced it to conform. This decision weighed heavily on me, and it's something I wish I could go back and change.

Later, the same coworker who had expressed discomfort revealed deeper issues. As a young woman in charge of the work center, my authority was often questioned. My peer, upset by my position, showed resistance and undermined my leadership. His resentment grew when I reported his unprofessional behavior, resulting in his first write-up.

This experience taught me a profound lesson about the importance of staying true to oneself. Conforming to make others comfortable can come at the cost of losing one's voice and identity. It also underscored the biases and challenges Latina women face in leadership roles, where cultural and gender prejudices can intersect.

By reflecting on this moment, I found the strength to embrace my heritage and assert my identity proudly. It's a journey of reclaiming my voice and power, not just for myself but for all Latina women who navigate similar challenges. This experience fuels my commitment to supporting women veterans through my nonprofit organization, SIS, ensuring that they, too, can find and use their voices in a world that often asks them to conform.

As we fight to change the stereotype of what Latino work looks like, we must remain steadfast in our identity and our mission to uplift others.

Leonor Branch is a trailblazer with a rich background in service, leadership, and community empowerment background. Raised in Chicago by parents who immigrated from Mexico for a better life, Leonor became the first woman in her family to join the military and earn a college degree. After 20 years of service as a mother of three in the military, she retired and embarked on a journey to find her identity and voice as a community leader. As a fitness coach at the YMCA and founder of Sisters in Service-Greater St. Louis (SIS), Leonor is passionate about empowering women veterans. She is a proud member of prestigious nonprofit organizations like The Mission Continues, Rotary Club, Toastmasters International, the O'Fallon-Shiloh Chamber of Commerce, and Veterans of Foreign Wars (VFW). Leonor believes that bringing diversity to a team often means being the only one who looks like you so that others can follow. Her mission is to inspire and lead others in the pursuit of their dreams.

Contact information for Leonor can be accessed here.

Dr. Gabriela Romero

Leave the Prison of Your Mind

"Let yourself be loved," she said, "you deserve to be loved." *La Prima, La Iniciada*, had mentioned three urgent messages that first day of February of 2023; the one about love was the first message she heard when the portal opened. The second message was about communication; "*tenés que decir lo que sentís*," she commanded. "Say how you feel, say it all. If you don't express yourself, words die inside you and hurt you. Release it all, the good and the bad." We had been trying to free my fifth chakra, so that I could reveal my inner being and buried emotions. But it was hard. In a later sacred cacao ceremony, I choked and struggled to breathe while *La Prima Iniciada* rushed to help me. I was healing. Although it would still take time for me to truly open up and decode the ancestral calling.

Growing up, I saw the woman I wanted to become in parts and pieces of my female ancestors and my mother, who was the "first intellectual light in my life," as my doctoral thesis dedication would read later. I knew I had a knack for public speaking, for sharing, for connecting. My dad taught me rhetoric and recitation, and although I wasn't going to be a *gaucho recitador* like him, we did share that child prodigy aura. I knew, however, that "*en boca cerrada no entran moscas*," and that if I was to avoid trouble, I'd better stay quiet, lest my words seal my fate. *La hija mayor. El ejemplo.* I was the eldest of four, and my sacred duty was to be my siblings' role model. My doom was perfection and nothing less. When that accident happened when I was 19, I took full responsibility. I was supposed to be perfect, and I failed. I couldn't care for a child; I caused pain. It didn't matter that everyone saw it for what it was, an unfortunate domestic accident. It didn't matter that the chain of events that caused that pot of boiling water to fall on his little body was not my responsibility. I was supposed to know and do better. It was my fate to be my siblings' model.

I lived up to that expectation and then some. I finished with the highest scores in college while working full-time and completed my degree in record time. I buried myself in work and endless hours of studying while the Argentine economy collapsed, my savings drained into nothingness, and my father struggled with the loss of a job yet again. I remember that day when the officers came to repossess the last vehicle the family had as a source of income… all I could do was shut the door to my room and study. The sooner I accrued college credits, the sooner I could work as a teacher. By the time I finished my degree, I kept three jobs and was sleeping only four hours a day. My dad had managed to purchase a motorcycle now, with which we would ride to college when I had an important exam, so I wouldn't have to wait for the bus. The determination to finish my degree with the best marks earned me a scholarship as an exchange student to the United States, which was a step closer to my actual dream: *un doctorado de los Estados Unidos*. Alas, there were no resources available to even get started. The family didn't have money for a plane ticket. My three jobs were not enough. However, challenges didn't halt my pursuit. I had not yet begun my year as an exchange student, but I already saw my Doctoral diploma in hand. I relied on my inner certainty, the love of my family, and the guidance of my ancestors.

"Do you know how many people complete a PhD worldwide?" my therapist asked only three years later. By then, I was struggling with extreme anxiety and depression trying to make it work so badly... "Less than 2 percent." How many of those PhDs are women who must straddle their domestic and intellectual lives, I wondered...but I was resolute to achieve my professional goals *and* raise a family. I wanted to be a mother. As I completed that dissertation riddled with anxiety, sprinkled with depression, and overtaken by loneliness, I centered it around the knowledge that I would raise independent, caring, capable women who would accomplish anything they desired hard enough. Just like their mother.

I pushed through for the sake of my daughters, my own sake, and that of the women in my life, uplifting and guiding me. I was emotionally isolated. I had become numb in that process of survival and perfection-seeking I had been compelled to live in for decades. I had no room for creativity, only doing, and the webs of words stayed trapped in my throat. PhD, checked. First job, checked. Promotion, checked. I was now a single mother and was looking for something I could not describe. There was an uneasiness in me, a gut feeling that I was in the wrong space, that my life was being lived only halfway, that I wasn't fulfilling my soul. Healing, like grieving, isn't linear, so I hunted for answers everywhere and paid close attention to the signs. I asked my grandparents for a signal about my new path, a revelation. Just like they had guided me before, I needed them to counsel me forward now. The messages that my cousin *La Iniciada* had shared were "urgent." "These are messages you need to hear now," she said. "Let yourself be loved; express yourself; leave the prison of your mind."

How can a seemingly exemplary professional and mother "express herself" and "leave the prison of her mind?" The fear of judgment paralyzed me. But sometimes, the path finds *you*. I eventually understood that healing and revealing were interweaved threads of my life's journey. "*Tenés que decir lo que llevás dentro.*" There was so much I knew and witnessed that I had never articulated to anyone. I had been numbed far too long; fight or flight, survival mode. Not anymore. Now it was time to pause and observe. Take note, and embrace; act, albeit imperfectly. The sign from my ancestors was clear: Speak. So I did. I relied on the support of my grandparents and "let myself be loved." The opposite of love is fear, and fear had stricken and silenced me for years.

This is a story of resilience amidst an incredibly isolating immigrant experience, one in which deteriorating mental health took front stage. Only immigrant women trying to keep a family together and succeed professionally recognize the mental weight of needing to do everything perfectly or risk total loss. I acknowledge now the generative power of my legacy. My daughters can see a woman who overcame the odds. I saw the end, so I created it. From a small Argentine city, I saw that I had a doctoral degree, so it happened. They see a woman who kept her intellectual dream intact while caring for them and offering them the best of both worlds: the opportunities that only this land can provide, and the values that came from our Italian and Argentine backgrounds. The steps that went into that process were co-created by my mind, my soul, and the Universe; sheer determination. Synchronicity is the mother of all signs. *Las cosas pasan cuando tienen que pasar.* I had to live those twenty-something years learning to be better, to give better during the rest of my life. Twenty-five years of trauma are not easy to unwind...The synchronicity with which I embarked on a new life, embraced the death of the old and transformation into the new, allowed myself to enjoy time and luxury and love and sensuality, and was thrusted into the baring of my own wounds was unparalleled. A timing so wonderfully synchronized by the Universe, that I, the grand planner, could not have scheduled it more precisely myself.

Our guides who have passed on enjoy sending us coins to let us know they are with us. I know my grandfather is with me; I didn't need to hear it from *La Prima Iniciada*. I knew it when I drove to my first trauma therapy session on April 17 and saw that quarter on the ground as soon as I opened my car door. It was his undeniable assurance that I was on the right path. The dancer on the coin is suspended on a leap, sustained by unknown forces, propelled by her own strength, dynamically dancing forever on that silver coin. *Gracias, abuelo.* I get it. I need to leap forward and face it all head-on in a beautiful dance of strength and pain and effort and repetition, just like the ballerina on the coin. Wounds were opened, and they were raw. But the pus and blood that is oozing out is leaving room for new life.

I am at a new crossroads now, and although I might flounder, I remind myself of my endurance. "*¿Quién te dijo que lo nuevo que buscás no te ha llegado ya?*" he asks lovingly. I ignore how the story ends. As a child, I would read the ending of novels right away to be able to savor the rest of the narrative with the knowledge of the conclusion. Now, I co-create. I read as I write, so I cannot ascertain what the ending holds, only that it is perfect, even if I am not. It is a journey of reacquaintance with my voice, which stifled for far too long while creating beings, fleeing the inevitable, and pursuing perfection is now finding timid spouts of release. My voice will no longer seal my fate; my voice will free it. I have left the prison of my mind.

Dr. Gabriela E. Romero, originally from Mendoza, Argentina, has lived in the United States for over 20 years. She is a committed community member, educator, and humanities practitioner. She completed her graduate studies at Washington University in St. Louis, where she obtained a Ph.D. in *Hispanic Languages and Literatures*. She also holds a degree in *English and Teacher Training* from Universidad Nacional de Cuyo in Mendoza. She is currently a professor and department head at Lindenwood University, where she designs and teaches courses in English, Spanish, Gender Studies, and Hispanic and LatinX literature and culture. She has presented her work domestically and abroad, published in peer-reviewed journals, and received awards in teaching and writing. Her work has been supported by organizations such as the National Endowment for the Humanities Summer Institute. She loves working out and spending time with her two daughters.

Contact information for Gabriela can be accessed here.

Tania Interian

Finding Your Voice

Finding your voice is always a challenge. You must discover what is your voice, what is your passion, and what is your purpose. There is no defined age when this happens. We are always on that journey, even though we are not aware of it.

Many times during my childhood and teen years, I came to the United States for vacations with my family to Las Vegas, Orlando, and California. In the year 2000, I moved to St. Louis from Mexico City to support my new husband, who was pursuing a job offer. This time it was a more radical move to live here. I did not know what life would be like, but I was young and full of optimism.

I had earned a law degree in Mexico and had professional aspirations that I could follow there. I already had a full-time job and was living independently by myself for a few years, but the move to the United States changed all that. It came very quickly.

We were married in August 2000, and we were not even living together at that time as I was already living by myself. We found a home that we were planning to rent together and began renovations on that house before moving there when he told me he accepted a job offer to come work in St. Louis, Missouri. I never wanted to pursue living in the United States as I already had a fulfilling life in my home country.

My law degree in Mexico did not count for anything in the United States, and I quickly found out that my migratory status did not allow me to work here legally. This was disheartening as I was an independent woman in my home country, but I had to accept my new reality at that time. Soon after arriving, I found out I was pregnant. In 2001, we had our first child. Not being able to work was frustrating as it suppressed participating and having a voice in my new world.

In 2004 I had my second child. Although I was happy with my girls, I was still very frustrated to not be able to work. Our marriage started to have many problems, mostly financial. We started dating when we were very young. We were raised with very different ideas about the woman's role in the family, plus the fact that we never lived together even though we dated for eight years in Mexico. Reality hit when we started living together in the United States.

I was raised with a strong conviction to be independent and to break the patterns of a typical Mexican family where the wife stays at home. My father always encouraged me to become financially and emotionally independent, so being unable to work here was a low blow for me.

I volunteered at organizations where my language skills and passion for helping people could be used. I volunteered at C.A.S.A. (Court Appointed Special Advocates) and at the Family Justice Center of St. Louis. This helped me meet other people and understand the different realities here in the United States. Still, without the possibility of working "legally" here, with a broken marriage and in tremendous need of financial stability, I resorted to re-selling items on eBay. That was not enough. My options at the moment were:

1. Cleaning houses, but I was scared of being accused of stealing, so I passed on that.

2. Babysitting, but what if something happened to the kid… so I passed on that as well.

3. Waitressing in a restaurant, and that was my best option back then.

I did not have experience waiting tables, but I learned. I didn't have the best experience with the employer as he was the true definition of a boss and not a leader. I knew that was my best option at the moment, and I got the most out of it as I could. I had a need to support myself and allow my daughters to be involved in extracurricular activities. This experience showed me the reality of many people who hold professional degrees in their country and are not able to work legally in this country due to the economic and security issues in their home countries.

The day I received my work permit, a new world opened for me. It was exciting and terrifying at the same time, as I had not worked in a professional field in many years. I applied to entry level jobs, but soon realized that my law degree disqualified me for many jobs. They said that I was overqualified. I stopped mentioning that on applications and interviews.

I was looking for something meaningful to do. I wanted more than just a job. I wanted to be able to utilize my Spanish skills and be able to help people. Finally, in 2008 I got the opportunity I was hoping for. I would be working as a team member for an agent of a large national insurance company. My job was to focus on the Hispanic community for their insurance needs. Getting the proper certifications in the state was a challenging requirement to keep the job. I was so hungry and desperate for stability and autonomy that I got the certifications quickly. With broken English and a lot of hunger, I started one of the best journeys of my life.

I became aware of the need for a Spanish-speaking insurance agent to provide service to the underserved Hispanic community. The leadership in the company also saw this. While my career began as an employee of another agent, I began working my way toward opening my own agency.

I worked for three years as a staff member until I was selected by this large national insurance company in 2011 to complete a two-and-a-half-year training process to become an independent contractor and agency owner. This was a rigorous and highly selective process. I had to prove to the company through different competencies that I would be a long-time, productive, and engaged insurance agent, along with many other licenses I had to acquire.

Finally, in August 2013, the doors of Tania Interian Agency opened. The company made it subject to a one-year probation contract. I had to prove, with high production goals and leadership competencies, managing a business and a team, that I could be a worthy long-time and elite insurance agent for this large insurance company. At the time of the opening, I was recently divorced and emotionally broken with a level of stress that I don't wish for anyone.

Opening an agency represented a hard financial commitment and risk. I had to invest the little money I had saved and take out additional loans for this opportunity. Risking all I had, this was my best chance to obtain independence and a bright future for my daughters. Returning to my home country was no longer an option, even though, in my lowest moments, I wanted to run back to Mexico. That would mean starting again from zero. I didn't want to put my daughters through more change as they were the ones who inspired me to keep fighting through all the hardships for this amazing professional opportunity to become a business owner, to be able to provide for them financially, and to be a role model for them.

I had many other professional challenges that would arise with the opening of my agency. Some of them came to me as a complete shock. I realized that people with whom I had close working relationships were now the people trying to boycott or block me from advertising my agency. I had to face professional organizations that were supposed to support

Latino business owners who didn't support me and gave me the cold shoulder. I also discovered that although my English was professionally proficient by now, I still had to face many comments and insults due to my accent and my heritage. This would have discouraged many other people, but I knew I had to keep fighting and moving forward to be a voice on behalf of my Latino community that did not have a voice yet.

Despite these barriers, I need to mention that there were many fantastic people who came out of nowhere in my life to extend their support emotionally and professionally. They wanted to pay forward the goodwill that they themselves experienced when they were starting out. Others simply believed in the vision, passion, and mission of my agency as the first Latina of this large insurance company in the state of Missouri, and they became my customers. I kept moving forward and focused on building my business through educating and giving back to my community and always looking out for their best interest.

I would like to leave a legacy for all women who are currently facing challenges to know that with passion and determination, you can also break the pattern of economic and emotional dependency to create a better life for yourself and your children and become a role model of autonomy for all of them.

Born in Mexico City, Mexico, Tania was the second of four children. She earned her law degree in Mexico and worked there as an attorney until she moved to the United States. Tania worked as a volunteer at C.A.S.A. (Court Appointed Special Advocates) and for the Family Justice Center.

In 2008, Tania started her career at State Farm. In 2013, she opened the doors to Tania Interian Agency. Her team of bilingual professionals share her passion for educating the community.

She has served on the board of the Latino Roundtable of Southwestern Illinois. Tania is actively involved in the community and is always looking for ways to give back and strengthen the community she lives and works in.

Outside of work, Tania enjoys spending time with her husband and her two beautiful daughters, who are always the inspiration for everything she does, as well as her rescued dogs, Lola and George.

Contact information for Tania can be accessed here.

Estephanina Martinez

The Healing Journey:
Reconciling the Past, Building a New Future

Impetus of Change

What are you no longer willing to endure? What are you willing to do to change your quality of life? For my maternal great-grandparents and my father, it meant leaving everything behind to seek an unknown future in the United States. They fled poverty and dangerous conditions with little money, no education, and no English. That legacy led to hundreds of births, the pursuit of the American Dream, and, a generation later, a significantly improved quality of life with higher levels of education.

When the pressure is great enough, it forces change. My great-grandparents risked their lives crossing the Rio Grande, facing the uncertainty of not being accepted into society and lacking basic needs like food or shelter. Similarly, my father left Puerto Rico at 22. I found myself making a similar move at the same age, just a few states away. I joined my only sibling, my older sister.

My Mexican great-grandparents and my Puerto Rican father settled in the same Hispanic neighborhood, in the same city, in the same four-plex apartment, where my parents eventually met. My mother, raised by her grandparents, befriended my uncle and his wife. A photo of her made its way back to Puerto Rico, where my father, upon seeing it, felt love at first sight. Determined to make her his wife, he saved money as a street mechanic and made arrangements with his brother.

This was during a time when industrialized jobs were booming in the Northern States, attracting low-educated, low-skilled immigrant workers. These sweltering factory jobs offered my father, with only a sixth-grade education, an opportunity to earn significantly more than he could in Puerto Rico. When my sister and I decided to move away from home, my dad said, "Good. You have to go where the opportunities are."

When Opportunity Knocks

Being unfamiliar with the demographics of the Great Lakes region, people are often surprised that I grew up in Wisconsin. Born in Wisconsin, we were immersed in a Hispanic population three times that of St. Louis, where my sister and I settled. Here, we struggled to find a sense of community.

Despite this, there seemed to be more opportunities here. I found a niche, utilizing my license from Wisconsin to become a supervisor at an upscale spa. Later, I returned to my roots as an orthopedic massage therapist. I established and grew a massage therapy department alongside the Doctor of Chiropractic. My clients were impressed and urged me to start my own company. With just 33 clients promising to follow me, I took a leap of faith. I built my own company.

Within a year, I had overflowing clientele and hired part-time practitioners to assist. Being only one of two specialized massage therapists in the city, I received many referrals. A local physical therapy practice owner offered me a spot in his practice. His office continued to expand, and another opportunity presented itself. My business expanded from a staff of two to a staff of seven.

Winds of Change

The winds of change are always blowing. Despite my successes and growth, I was blindsided twice. First, the physical therapy owner informed me that they had been undercharging my rent and suddenly increased my monthly fee by over 70 percent. Then, they told me they were leaving our shared office space and would not have space for my growing practice. They were moving out in two months.

I scrambled to find a place for myself and my staff to work. I found a temporary space in the same building while our permanent space was being renovated. However, less than two years after moving in, we were hit by the global pandemic. With no clear guidance, I made the difficult decision to close the office indefinitely.

At that time, my body was completely burnt out. My reputation as the best massage therapist in St. Louis was a double-edged sword. My clientele refused to see my staff, even though I had enough clients for nearly three full-time practitioners. My staff had enough clients to keep them busy, but I had more than I could handle.

I had been overextending myself, offering 20 sessions a week and scheduling clients an entire year in advance. My clients knew that if they didn't schedule a standing appointment, it could take months to get back on my calendar. By March 2020, I was fully booked nine months in advance, leaving no room for new clients. My body said, "No more." I woke up with bilateral radiculopathy—nerve impingement starting in my neck, with symptoms traveling down both arms and hands.

Some mornings, I woke up with paralyzed arms. I knew I had to retire from massage. Convincing my clients to transfer to another practitioner proved difficult, and with the pandemic causing fear and isolation, my touch-based business model was unsustainable.

Healing and Recovery

Most people only rest when they are forced to. I was no exception. I had built a successful business, but my body had reached its breaking point. The decision to close my office and retire from massage was both uncertain and liberating. This was not the first time that my health had forced rest and recuperation.

When I was 13 years old, I contracted mononucleosis, with restrictions to only attend school every other day for half days. This first encounter with a health issue led me down a path of self-discovery that laid the foundation for my future career. The doctors advised me to rest, listen to my body, drink plenty of fluids, and eat healthy food. Being home so much, I found public television channels that showcased seated yoga, leading me to explore mindfulness, philosophy, and self-help.

The second time was after uterine surgery in December 2018. Healing from this surgery brought up hidden traumas. I experienced anger, severe depression, pain, and complex trauma triggers. Hypnotherapy with a licensed therapist uncovered memories of childhood molestation.

The uterus is part of the energy center called the Sacral Chakra. Here, emotions from ages 8 to 14 are stored. My abuse had started much earlier, but there was also some trauma that contributed to my trauma response. Also known as our "creative center," our Chakra, when in balance, helps us to feel safe within our bodies and environment.

Feeling unsafe at home and in my body was a childhood-long experience due to my dad's alcoholism and abuse and family migration. I felt unsafe because my sister had been kicked out at the age of 15. Our household resources were strained as my parents worked two jobs each and provided resources to our relatives. I became malnourished and developed an unhealthy relationship with food that lasted well into adulthood.

As I worked to heal from these traumas, I realized that I had spent much of my life operating from a place of fear. These fears had been ingrained in me from a young age and had shaped my approach to life and work. Healing from these wounds allowed me to see the patterns that had been driving me and to begin the process of unwinding them.

Reconciling the Past, Building a New Future

My journey has been more than professional success; it has been about reconciling my past and healing deep wounds. I have come to understand that my path as a healer was shaped not only by the skills and techniques, but by the traumas I experienced and overcame. This allowed me to guide others on their paths to healing.

In my practice, I use the "Old Ways"—a blend of ancestral wisdom, natural healing, and blend in modern techniques and tools. This helps others connect with nature, heal traumas, and align with their soul's purpose. It is deeply rooted in my heritage, drawing on the knowledge of my first mentor, David "Eight Eagles," a medicine man originally from the Tigua Tribe of El Paso, Texas. I met him when he worked as a teacher at the local Indigenous School.

He, just like my Tex-Mex grandmother, had to assimilate to survive and wasn't taught the culture spanning just one or two generations back. Since my grandmother didn't raise my mother, that knowledge didn't get passed on for a couple of generations. Somehow, I knew. My dad's mother was the village midwife and healer. "She knew how to use all the plants," Dad said. It was a light bulb moment. Not only did I look just like her, but I was carrying forward her legacy to use my ancestral wisdom to intuitively help others heal.

This has served me as I provided a range of services that help people identify patterns that aren't serving them. It replaces them with new tools and techniques to self-manage their health. Community demand also led me to host community mindfulness, creative, and support group events. Those desiring to reconnect with their culture, nature, natural cycles of life, or the "old ways" of Indigenous Healing take my Shamanic Healing Mentorship courses.

Today, I am proud to offer this healing work to others, knowing that it is a beautiful and fulfilling path. If you feel called to join me on this journey, I invite you to take the first step and embrace the opportunity for change. Just as my great-grandparents, father, and I did, you have the power to forge a path of courageously pursuing a better life.

Estephanina has a diverse heritage and a lifelong passion for the arts and healing. This interest led her to train at Lakeside School of Massage Therapy and with a medicine man in Southeastern Wisconsin. She has 20-plus years in the wellness industry and launched a pain-relief practice, Ortho Touch Therapy, in 2010. What started as a solo practice turned into a thriving multi-practitioner wellness center. Since closing the center, she is poised to launch La Unica Wellness in the fall of 2024 to host her hybrid courses for those seeking to find their purpose and reconnect with ancient traditions. Next winter, she will begin teaching a Foundational Touch and Techniques class for a local massage therapy school.

Estephanina completed the Inner City Capital Connection Mini-MBA program in 2023 and the Hispanic Leadership Initiative in 2019. She is also a member of the Associated Bodywork and Massage Professionals (ABMP), "Women Who Drum," Lakota Inipi Group, and "Friends of the Hummingbirds" Community.

Contact information for Estephanina can be accessed here.

LeAnna Bailon

Who Am I?

*"The woman that starts the race is not
the same woman that finishes the race."*
-Unknown

My *Abuelo*, a carpenter from Manta, Ecuador, arrived in New York City
as a tourist in the late 60s. While there, he overheard others talking about
visas, so he encouraged my *Abuela* to apply for one. My *Abuela*, a seam-
stress, successfully obtained the visa and was able to bring the rest of her
family. Mom immigrated on a student visa.

Dad joined the U.S. Army in November 1975 and was stationed at
various duty stations throughout his career, eventually choosing to settle
in Alabama. He retired after 26 years of service. Our summer vacations
were spent with our paternal or maternal *abuelos* in the Bronx or Ecuador.
I was 13 years old when my mom passed away. It was hard; she was loving,
caring, beautiful, joyful, selfless, and strong. Mom was deeply involved in
the Latino community, organizing numerous events until she passed away
from ovarian cancer at 41. My family, especially my paternal side, calls me
"Negra" or *"Negrita"* as a sign of endearment. I'm the youngest of three.
My brother, who currently serves in the U.S. Army, is married with four

beautiful daughters. My sister, who suffered a brain stem injury at 21 in a 1999 car accident, recently passed away. Her 26-year-old daughter works in the medical field.

At 21, uncertain about continuing college nursing school and mindful of my dad's financial sacrifices, I decided to enlist in the U.S. Air Force, searching for a more meaningful path in life. I had planned to join with my cousin, but she enlisted six months earlier.

I went to basic training in the summer of 2001, facing intense heat and humidity. I suffered an injury that temporarily removed me from physical training and led to a medical hold for physical therapy. Training continued at a slower pace, and I often called my dad in tears, wanting to quit. He encouraged me to push through, and after completing therapy, I passed my final physical test, I returned to my flight and graduated.

At technical school, during routine duties, 9/11 occurred. I walked into the dayroom and saw the Twin Towers being hit on TV. Shock and disbelief washed over me—it felt unreal. Panicked, I tried calling my family in New York, but the lines were jammed. Fear and worry set in as we were immediately put on military lockdown, the sudden realization of the gravity of the situation sinking in as we secured our dorms and prepared for the unknown, what every soldier faces when war looms on the horizon.

Orders sent me to Royal Air Force Lakenheath, England. Along the way, I made lifelong friends. They became my family, and I'm still blessed to have them in my life 20-plus years later. In 2002, I was deployed to a forward operating base in Kuwait for a 60-day mission as part of Operation Southern Watch, a staging mission for possible large-scale operations in Iraq. As time went on, my orders were extended, lasting nearly six months. My peacetime duties were supplanted by wartime responsibilities. There was no escaping the constant tension and hypervigilance required as we provided supervised escort for nationals as they worked. The sand-choked, lung-burning desert heat and stench from trash and urinals were inescapable.

Once, while on an office food run, I was temporarily reassigned from my usual third-country national (TCN) duties to handle administrative tasks. I'll never forget that first piercing wail of the air-raid siren—my adrenaline spiked, and muscle memory took over: gas mask on, chem suit donned, take cover. Breathing became even more unbearable, sweat pooled inside my suit, and my vision became increasingly limited. As days passed, sirens were common, and we wore chemical suits 24/7. Being on alert meant forgoing hygiene for extended periods.

After Kuwait, I was assigned to Tinker Air Force Base in Oklahoma, a welcome relief from a war-torn country. As the war persisted, I deployed again, this time to Afghanistan, serving as the Admin for the Public Affairs office, working closely with an Army National Guard unit from Hawaii. The female soldiers were incredible, treating me like one of their own battle buddies. We lived near the Embassy compound. We could hear the relentless attacks—rapid gunfire. The days of traveling in unarmored vehicles, in the open country, our weapons at the ready were the most harrowing.

Returning from Afghanistan, with much relief, I recognized I was easily startled by noises and sudden movements, even rattled when routines were disrupted. Panic set in often for no reason I could justify, and I avoided large gatherings. To feel safer, I always chose a specific spot where I could be more vigilant. I sought help, and I attended counseling. I applied for a Base of Preference and chose Eglin Air Force Base (AFB), Florida. For the first time in six years, I would live near my family.

Dad, my rock and source of stability, accompanied me, as he did for all my moves, on the drive from Tinker AFB, Oklahoma, to Eglin AFB, Florida. During this assignment, my third deployment contingency orders could have sent me overseas. Luckily, I remained in Tampa, Florida, working as a support personnel admin. It was here that I chose motherhood. My son, Isaias, is now 15 years old. He has been the driving force for me to continue to strive to do better in everything I do and leave a legacy for him. My military service became a long-term career choice, just as my father had chosen.

The assignment to the University of Notre Dame was particularly challenging, as I found myself in an entirely civilian environment with no military resources to lean on. Among strangers, with Isa, a toddler, and being separated from my natal family was daunting. Choosing Growing Kids Learning Center was one of the best decisions I made. Though we don't stay in touch daily, the staff continues to follow my son's growth through social media and remember him fondly. The connections we formed, including our newly found Notre Dame family—Nana and Papa—and the holidays we spent together, hold a special place in our hearts. Becoming a single mother in the military brought challenges I never anticipated.

After four years, I chose to be reassigned near my brother in Washington state, allowing Isa and me to be surrounded by family so he could grow and bond with his cousins. I was deployed once more; this was six months to Turkey and my first separation from Isa. Thankfully, it was my last deployment and separation from my son.

On returning to Washington, my and my brother's orders coincided, both to Virginia. Dad joined us for the move, traveling for eight days from coast to coast.

I was assigned to the Pentagon for three years, but my time there was cut short after I requested a reassignment. Although I typically do not back down from challenges, I felt it was in my best interest to request reassignment due to ongoing difficulties with a civilian employee. I endured a year in this toxic environment, along with my coworkers, under consistent mistreatment. I was reassigned to the Contracting Squadron in Maryland for less than a year.

My new assignment was to Scott AFB, Illinois, as a Community Support Admin. It was here, as Isa was transitioning from middle school to high school, that I decided it was time to retire in October 2022. In my entire military career, I always had the support of my father, brother, sister-in-law, close friends, and my son's father, who supported my choice to remain single, become a mom, and pursue a career choice that often is not a viable choice for single parenting.

My father is my role model, teaching me invaluable lessons through his every action. He embodies personal strength, perseverance in difficult times, unwavering loyalty, and a rare compassion that many men struggle to express. His commitment and resilience in the face of immense loss are evidence of his enduring love and strength—qualities I aspire to emulate. He stood by my mother from the moment she fell ill until her last breath and remained at my sister's side every day for 24 years, ensuring she received the care she needed. Even now, he visits her gravesite daily. The values I hold dear are deeply rooted in the example set by the man who raised me after my mother passed away.

Life is filled with obstacles and unique challenges, but it's not only how we overcome them that shapes who we are—it's also the people we share our lives with. Family and lasting friends have helped me appreciate every step of my journey and find contentment in where I am today. This is who I am.

LeAnna Marie Bailon is a first-generation Latina, born in Fort Bragg, North Carolina, a military brat moving around the first six years of her life, then growing up in Southeast Alabama. She followed the same path as her father and joined the U.S. Air Force, served 21 years, and retired.

LeAnna holds an associate degree in Information Management. She has experience in knowledge management, administration, and communication. She currently works as a Senior Technical Writer for Diligent Consulting.

Contact information for LeAnna can be accessed here.

Mayra Taylor Garcia

De Aquí y de Allá

Am I *more* Mexican than American?

Am I *more* American than Mexican?

A common phrase in Latino culture to describe the shared experience of not feeling like you can claim one or the other is *Ni de aqui Ni de alla*. Neither from here. Nor from there. As a child and adolescent, I did feel like that phrase resonated with my experience. No matter where I was, people I encountered wanted to tell me that I was from the other country.

I am Mexican, and reluctantly, I am American. Let me explain. I was born in Mexico and am proud of my roots and culture. Like many millennial immigrants, I have spent more of my life here in the United States than in my birth country.

As a young child, it was obvious that I was not from the United States. I didn't know English when I started kindergarten. That experience is defining for a 5-year-old child: not knowing what the teacher was saying, just trying to follow the lead. I learned English quickly and was fully integrated into the general education classes within two years, but that did not make me feel like I belonged. I have always had straight black hair and brown skin, and as I got older, the question was, "Are you illegal?"

As a girl in elementary school, I internalized that I was not from here and asked myself, "Do I even belong here?"

As a teenager, I spent several summer breaks in Mexico with my sisters. Two whole months with our grandparents is an experience I am deeply grateful for today. It allowed me to stay immersed in my home country's culture, Spanish, and spend time with family that I didn't see regularly. My cousins call me *gringa*, referring to the fact that I was "from" the United States. The hardest thing for me was hearing the words "*Hablas español con acento americano...ya no eres de aquí.*" Those words dug deep. How could I not be from here if I was born here?

I went to college and didn't go back to Mexico for 10 years, busy with summer courses and internships. These years were the most transformative for me. I moved away from home; in fact, my family moved to a different state, I got my first job, and I learned how to be self-sufficient. I also credit my liberal arts education for broadening my perspective during this time.

I majored in Biology, but I was able to take history classes, and I even minored in Spanish. I wanted to connect more with my heritage language however, some of my classmates made it a point to tell me that I was "cheating the system" because I was a heritage speaker studying Spanish. That could not be any further than the truth. Yes, I was able to skip the introductory classes, but the higher-level classes made me work hard. I grew up learning Spanish orally, and that made writing Spanish difficult. I didn't know the rules of proper grammar until I learned phonetics formally through my courses. This was also the first time I immersed myself in literature written in Spanish with books such as *Mango Street* and *How the García Girls Lost Their Accents*.

As a woman in my early 20s, I had this *Ni de aqui Ni de alla* phrase in the back of my brain, but it didn't feel right. I am from Mexico. I was born there. I am proud of that. I am also from the United States. I grew up here, and I am thankful for the opportunities this country has afforded my family.

Recently I have seen the phrase change from *Ni de aqui Ni de alla* to *De aqui y de Alla.* This means "From here and from there." I finally feel a phrase that is more accurate to my experience. Two things can be true at the same time. I am *De aqui y de Alla.*

What solidified this for me was an experience I had at 30 years old. I was interpreting during an in-person meeting for my volunteer work. The health department was there discussing permits, among other things. They explained how they would use test strips as part of their inspection. As they were wrapping up the English portion, I was mentally running through all my Spanish, thinking, "How the heck do you say *test strips* in Spanish?" The reality was that I was out of time, and now it was my turn to repeat their words in Spanish. I had no other choice but to admit I didn't know how to say the "test strip," so I turned to the audience and asked for the words. They helped me out by saying, *"los test estrips."* We all collectively laughed, and I repeated, *"los test estrips."*

As I repeated the Spanish back, internally, I was having one of those movie moments where your whole life flashes before your eyes. I remembered various moments throughout my life that shaped me—my earliest memories at my third birthday party, walking into my kindergarten classroom not knowing English, practicing Mexican Folkloric Dancing, my quinceañera party, moving into my first apartment, getting married, giving birth to my children. I realized then and there that we are all *De aqui y de alla.* Sure, some people were born in the United States and don't know Spanish well. Some moved to the United States as adults and are more comfortable in Spanish. And some immigrants have never been back to their home country after coming to the United States as children. We were all our own variation of *De aqui y de alla.*

"Test strips" translates to *tiras reactivas,* but that doesn't matter. What matters is that at that moment, I realized that all people who are from and/or grow up in multiple cultures are living in duality, and there is nothing wrong with that. It is imperfect, and it is beautiful.

I have the privilege to travel back and forth between my two countries without fear. In the United States I have the opportunity to celebrate my Mexican heritage and put on the Hispanic Festivals in St. Louis, Missouri. I can translate back and forth to people who don't know the other language. I humbly take on the responsibility of advocating for immigrants and my Latine community. Had my parents not moved our family to the United States, I wouldn't have received the medical treatment I needed as a child, and I would not be who I am today. I can now own my "Mexicanness" at the same time that I own my "Americanness."

Along with my personal experiences, I have to credit many people for allowing me to get to this point in my journey. Authors such as Reyna Grande and Erika Sánchez have told their stories and gifted my generation with literature that resonates with our experience. Farzana Nayan wrote *Raising Multiracial Children: Tools for Nurturing Identity in a Racialized World.* This allowed me to reflect on my own upbringing as well as provided me with perspective on raising my own multiracial and multicultural children. My husband often jokingly says, "You all pick when you want to be Mexican, when you want to be American, and when you are Mexican American." That is true. Yes, depending on the context, my answer can change, and it's important to remember that this is also a privilege and honor to be both. We are only one or two generations removed from when immigrants didn't teach their children their home language. There was fear of discrimination, and assimilation was crucial to survival.

Now we can celebrate duality and know that you do not have to pick or lose one thing for the other.

I have found power in my voice on this topic. This is for my children, other immigrants, and descendants of immigrants who will inevitably live in a more multicultural society. I'm writing this as I enjoy my time with *familia* in Mexico, with my husband and children in the next room. I am proud of my Mexican heritage and culture. *Soy bien Paisa.* I am grateful for my lived experience as a naturalized American in the United States. Recently, I found myself in a conversation with family and friends in Mexico. A comment was made about how I am from over "there" now. My response was short and sweet *"y tambien de aqui."* I am also from here.

I have discovered the beauty of living in the duality of being from here and from there. It is an incredible discovery to find the place of knowing that I can enjoy my experience in both. That you are not less than because you are also something else at the same time. I go back to the questions from all my life:

Am I more Mexican than American?

Am I more American than Mexican?

Yo soy de aquí y de allá.

Mayra, originally from Mexico, considers herself a St. Louis, Missouri, transplant. Mayra is a wife, a mother, a daughter, a sister, a friend, and a community member. At 4 years old, she left Mexico with her mother, father, and younger sister. Having grown up in the United States, she had the privilege of living in five different states.

She aspired to be a doctor but ultimately decided against medical school. Instead, she became a high school biology teacher for St. Louis Public Schools. This shaped her understanding of the education system and its inequities. After four years of teaching, she transitioned to the nonprofit sector, focusing on equitable access to high-quality STEM learning and employment opportunities.

Outside of work, she is involved on the planning committee for the bi-annual Hispanic Festivals. She enjoys doing DIY projects, jogging at Forest Park, and spending time with her kids, Kurly III and Yaretzi, and her husband, Kurly Jr.

Contact information for Mayra can be accessed here.

Jessica Tapia

No Time to Give Up

My name is Jessica Tapia, and this is my story of strength, resilience, and perseverance when all else fails around me. It narrates how my faith in God and belief in the right things helped me overcome a few of the biggest obstacles I have faced. I was born in Pisco, Ica, Peru, and lived in that small town for about two decades. As a child, I always knew I wanted to do big things in life and become successful to stand on my own two feet. Life gave me precisely that, but not without many twists and turns.

My family and I moved to Lima in 1992, where I went to study to become a secretary of administration. I attended one of the best schools and started working for different government entities. I married my ex-husband in 2002 and moved to the United States the same year. Our marriage didn't last long; however, I am still grateful to have met him because the outcome resulted in my two beautiful children, John and Marcia.

I went to ESL (English as a Second Language), and as my English started improving, I started working cleaning some houses. I was not poor, but it was how I could make money later on when my English was much better. I found my first job selling tiles; I had to learn how to convert square meters to square feet and learn about the different materials and products the company sold. While I was working for this company, I got pregnant, so I quit and moved to work for May Company as a calling debt collector. I enjoyed my time there. Still, when I had my daughter in July 2005, I had to quit and became a stay-at-home mom.

In 2006, I went to real estate school and got my license as an agent. After working and learning about the process of buying and selling houses, I decided to go back to real estate school to get my broker license, and in 2012, I opened my own company. Being my own boss allowed me to meet all kinds of people, and I learned how to deal with everyone. Starting the business was not easy, but I made it happen.

In 2013, my ex-husband and I divorced, as we couldn't be together anymore. We fought all the time, and things started getting worse; for him, I was either worthless, too fat, or too something. In his eyes, I was good for nothing. I now realize that people's behavior reflects themselves, but at the time, my self-respect plummeted; I knew something wasn't right. I soon realized that I was married to a narcissist who never thought I was good enough, so it was best for us to be apart and move on with our lives. Ladies, don't *ever* think you aren't good enough for any man.

I was granted some of the properties we bought while we were married, and I had to refinance all of them, which I knew would be difficult as I had already checked with some lenders, and they had already told me no. I had only six months to refinance the property, including my own home, so my ex-husband would call me to tell me that I should give back the property, and he allowed me to keep my house. If I weren't able to refinance, then I would lose everything, including my own home, and possibly be homeless. I asked God to help me, and He did. He sent me someone who, after learning what I needed to do to keep my properties, told me not to worry because *God* was with us. That never happened.

Initially, things were difficult; I was on my own and had to be responsible for everything. I focused on my work as a broker/agent in real estate, and now it had to be 100 percent. I didn't have time to go out or have fun with friends because my priority was my kids. I needed to save the money to pay the bills, feed my kids, and do all that was required at the time. Sometimes, I had a very rough day, but "I didn't have time to give up!"

It was not easy. I couldn't show my kids that I was fighting depression. I would pretend that everything was fine. I didn't want to show how broken I was from the inside; even on my worst days, I smiled. I had some people to whom I used to refer at the time, such as my good friends or my kid's aunt, who abandoned and left me out of the group of friends I used to belong to. It was not easy, and sometimes I felt so lonely, especially when my kids went to their dad's house. Now I know I have been blessed. I understand going through everything made me stronger. God always had my back. I was finally reaching the end of the tunnel, and it seemed like all my hardships were worth it.

I know God works in many ways, but I never lost my faith. On the contrary, my faith was stronger every moment. Even though I said I felt alone, I knew I was never alone. I had surgery with some complications, and when my clients found out that I was recovering, they came to help my children and me. They showered me, cleaned my house, cooked, cared for my kids, did laundry, and much more. Being surrounded by all of them showed me that I was never alone. Many of these clients became close friends or family. My faith kept me closer to God in one way or the other.

I am so lucky because everyone I met and helped during my journey showed up for me when my family in Peru couldn't be there to help me. I don't give much credit to myself or my relationships with people. All the credit goes to God and how He opened doors for me that I didn't think were possible. My relationship with my clients continued and strengthened with time, and since I had a great rapport with them, I found a little community for myself.

My main goal was to help my Hispanic community find homes and start a new life. I knew that life could be challenging, and if I could help people, I felt like I was accomplishing something big. Since I was older than many of them, I considered myself a parent to them and counseled them in different matters whenever they required assistance.

I tried my best to be present for people both physically and emotionally because I know what it is like to be alone and not have anyone in your corner when you need them the most. It was a lonely and helpless feeling I wouldn't wish upon anyone.

After some time of being a single mother, I got married to my current husband. My husband was a friend whom I met in 1997 in my hometown. I reconnected with him in 2013, and we started our relationship in 2015. We got married in October 2017 in the United States. He has two sons, Joaquin and Gabriel, who live with us. Now I have a whole house; I am happier than ever. My husband Ricardo is my soulmate. He constantly shows me how much he loves me by everything he does for me, and he makes me laugh most of the time.

For anyone struggling to start something new, I would like to say that it is not easy, but possible. You have to believe in yourself and believe everything will be all right. Make sure to persist and never hesitate. If you think that I didn't feel down, you are mistaken. However, the difference was I never gave up on myself and pushed through. I still believe I have a long way to go, but with God holding my hand, I know everything will work out.

Jessica Tapia was born in Pisco, Ica, Peru, in 1973. In 1992, she moved to Lima, Peru, before coming to the United States in 2002. She currently enjoys her life in St. Louis with her husband and four children, Marcia and John, and Ricardo's sons, Joaquin and Gabriel.

She has worked in real estate since 2006. Working in real estate is her greatest passion. She likes being able to help people make it possible to own a home.

As a board member of Caring Ministers, she is deeply committed to empowering low-income families, immigrants, and refugees to achieve self-sufficiency and sustainable housing. This year, she completed her goal of becoming a Public Notary and Minister.

She is bilingual in English and Spanish, which is a significant advantage in her profession. She is dedicated to ensuring her clients feel at ease and well-informed throughout the process.

Contact information for Jessica can be accessed here.

Eileen Otero Wolfington

Embrace Who You Are, Even If You're an Outlier

outlier
noun: a person or thing that is atypical
within a particular group, class, or category
(Merriam-Webster Dictionary)

As a Latina in my late adulthood, I have some nuggets of wisdom that I wish to share. Perhaps one may resonate with you.

I grew up in a humble multicultural home environment in Milwaukee, Wisconsin. *Mami* was from Zacatecas, northwest of Mexico City. *Papi* was from the town of Cidra in the central region of Puerto Rico. I guess that makes me a Mexi-Rican American, three cultural identities that I've navigated for 68 years. During my pre-school childhood, Spanish was often spoken at home. Both of my parents had accents. My two sisters and I were immersed in the local traditional school system, where only English was spoken. That is why you don't detect an accent when I speak and why my Spanish isn't perfect. In fact, I was favorably complimented about my enunciation by an ESL educator when I taught English to Middle Eastern refugees. Because my married name is Wolfington, folks are often surprised when they meet me in person for the first time. They don't expect to see a Latina nor a woman with brown skin. It didn't hurt to be *morena* (dark) when I was young. Papi affectionately used terms of endearment by calling me his *prieta chula* (black cutie). However, during my youth, I became offended when people would ask me, "What are you?"

It's interesting how words that hurt me while growing up simply roll off my shoulders today. An intensive week-long workshop entitled *Dismantling Racism* educated me about racial issues and helped me to recognize my own biases. This life-changing experience inspired me to become a contracted diversity facilitator. For years, I aspired to be an advocate for the underserved, the marginalized, immigrants, refugees, minorities, and low-income non-minorities. Here in the United States, this was often a difficult task back then and in the current climate.

Most new folks that I've met during the past 10 years do not know that I had a 33-year consumer banking career. While in college, rather than major in education or social work as many of my Latino/Latina colleagues did, I chose to be an outlier, so I majored in Business. An incredible nonprofit called INROADS created a pathway for me to complete a four-year internship in banking. This resulted in a full-time job offer which I accepted. When I could afford them, I purchased suits and heels, and I wore my hair up for work almost every day. During the later years of my banking career, I was able to use my Spanish for the first time. What a joy it was to empower limited English-language speakers and many non-English speakers to open a bank account, apply for a loan, start a small business, or buy a home.

In 2010, I transitioned from the corporate arena to the nonprofit world. That's when I put away the suits and wore my hair down. Again, I felt like an outlier due to not having any type of health educational background. *(Please note, this was not a requirement for the job.)* I became a community health worker for a nonprofit clinic. Joyfully, I was able to use my Spanish not only with our patients, but also with many of my coworkers. I consider this experience the best informal introduction to the world of public health.

I learned about social determinants of health and the challenges faced by uninsured and underinsured immigrants and non-immigrants. I informally educated myself to learn as much as I could about exercise, nutrition, and the symptoms of undiagnosed diseases. I felt driven to educate and motivate our patients to begin to live a healthier lifestyle. I saw results with those who were compliant, but I wanted to reach more people.

Though I wasn't a trained professional in public health, nursing, or nutrition, I applied for a position to become a health and wellness program coordinator for a nonprofit social service agency. Yes, once more, I felt like an outlier. However, it was with great pleasure that I accepted the position to be in my dream job. I was tasked to facilitate exercise and nutrition education programming for predominantly Spanish-speaking women and other limited English-speaking immigrant women. How exciting it was to have a captive audience five days a week. This afforded the opportunity to help establish mutually agreed-upon goals with the participants to begin their journey of wellness.

Because I am a lifelong learner, during the past eight years, I began studying alternative forms of medicine and wellness practices to calm the mind, body, spirit, and soul. My hope was to offer these modalities to the Spanish-speaking and immigrant community when I retired in 2022. To my surprise, I was faced with unexpected resistance. In a culture where indigenous practices and *remedios caseros* (home remedies) were practiced by our ancestors, I felt confident that my offer to inspire balance and harmony would be embraced. It wasn't. However, I'm comfortable in accepting that the women who resonate with my self-care offerings are predominantly U.S. born, English-speaking participants who have affectionately embraced this outlier.

Having learned to *embrace* myself as an outlier has allowed me to live authentically and unapologetically during these remaining couple of decades of my life. Here's how you can too!

Educate yourself. Learn as much as you can because knowledge is power. Be curious. Ask questions. Find something that you love and enhance your skills. Dare to be different *(even if you become an outlier)*. Enrich your mind with enlightened thoughts and experiences. Eat nutritiously to do all the things that require energy. Use your personal empowerment to enable others. Eliminate your ego and become endearing to all.

Maintain a high level of integrity in all that you do. Motivate yourself to manifest positivity in your life. A daily practice of prayer and meditation will help you to manage through the difficult times. Magnify your life goals to achieve success. Become a role model for other women. May the legacy that you lead today be memorialized one day.

Be brave. Believe in yourself and remove all that no longer serves you. Learn breathwork to maintain a balanced and harmonious lifestyle. This will also give you a daily boost. Brighten the lives of others.

Radically accept the radiant woman that you are becoming. Be receptive to new opportunities that help you to renew and restore your body, mind, spirit, and soul. Recognize, resolve, and release negative thoughts. Respect all things human, including your relationship with the earth and all the natural resources that the earth provides. Rejoice and be grateful for the life you have been given. Rekindle your friendships with laughter and joy as you re-experience your inner child. Recite positive affirmations to refresh you each day. Ready yourself for new and exciting opportunities. Be true to yourself and *"keep it real."*

Affirm your beliefs and live each day abundantly. Be adventurous. Aspire to be the most amazing woman that you were destined to become. Your admirable qualities will inspire others to ambitiously seek out their own authenticity. Adapting to new experiences that reflect your personal values will bring attention to your positive attributes. Show your appreciation with affection. Actively incorporate positive thoughts, words, and actions to foster supportive behaviors. Assertively become a leader and mentor. Be accessible to young women who are attracted to your successful journey.

Collaborate. Be considerate of other women as you accompany them to amplify your collective voices. Celebrate your successes. Build a community of like-minded and creative women who wish to be connected. Care for yourself first so that you can comfortably care for others. Practice self-compassion. Consistently sustain your confidence by committing to a daily routine of calming practices. Confidently maintain a cheerful disposition during life's challenges while keeping in mind the following phrase: *"This too shall pass."* Captivate the hearts and minds of others through your strength in vulnerability. Do not feel obligated to conform to trends.

Embrace your cultural identity with excitement and enthusiasm for your mental and emotional well-being. Encourage your Latina sisters with words of kindness. Elevate your mind through research, books, and lifelong learning. Engage in activities that enrich your mind. Excel in all that you do to earn a respected and positive reputation. Be proud of your ethnicity. *(By the way, my signature is the flower I wear in my hair every day. As a performer of folkloric Mexican and Puerto Rican dance, I've always worn floral hair adornment. This is an intentional symbol of my ethnicity.)*

In your life, may you reach a point of enlightenment with an open mind, positive insights, a release from the ego, and a broad awareness around how to navigate cultural expectations. Blessings to you *amiga querida* (dear friend)!

La Morena

I am here to dance the dream
In my sacred human form.
To celebrate my uniqueness
And ask no other to conform.
-Jamie Sams

Eileen Otero Wolfington, M.Ed., retired as a physical wellness coordinator. Coupled with her previous work experience as a community health worker, Eileen uses her gifts to motivate others to live in harmony in mind, body, spirit, and soul. She is a certified laughter yoga teacher and a Veriditas-certified labyrinth facilitator. She practices healing touch and energy medicine, grief movement, grief education and support, guided sound baths, and facilitated drum circles. Her hobbies include studying complementary forms of medicine, death, dying, and end-of-life education. She has a BA from the University of Wisconsin–Whitewater and an M.Ed. from the University of Missouri–St. Louis. She has been happily married to Daniel for 38 years.

Contact information for Eileen can be accessed here.

Gabriela Claudia Ochoa

Corajuda

Corajuda is a Spanish term that has followed me all my life, but I only cared to know a little about the word beyond its obvious implications. I knew it was something negative, a trait unbecoming of a young lady *proceeds to clutch pearls*. It wasn't until a recent moment of curiosity led me to look up the word that I discovered its other English meanings: brave, gutsy, and bold. This revelation ignited a fresh wave of anger. How had I spent years feeling maligned under a label that also held such powerful, positive connotations? That I'd been given half the truth? Society often dictates that young women should embody demureness and compliance, yet here I was, none of those things.

Growing up, I was nicknamed *corajuda*, which I was told translated into English as short-tempered. This, of course, was more upsetting to me because we weren't a Spanish-speaking family. Initially, my parents never found my attitude charming, unlike most adults who find a petulant and sassy child amusing. "Ugh, you're so *corajuda*. Why are you like this?" they would say in Spanglish, annoyed by my demeanor. There is no denying it; they were right—I was too easily irritated, and there was no straightforward reasoning behind my attitude. My defensiveness was often wrongly mistaken for shyness, and instead, I created a preemptive barrier against anticipated disappointments from those I feared would let me down. This behavior, rooted deeply in my fear of rejection for not fitting neatly into the expectations of my Latina identity, was something I only began to unpack and understand after years of therapy.

My perceived complex identity is likely a result of my upbringing in a household led by an active-duty Marine father and a career-driven mother. Our family often stood out as the only Latino family in our suburban California neighborhood. We looked the part, but our lifestyle didn't align with what I had imagined the traditional Latino experience to be. There were no large family gatherings, our holidays were quieter, and our home vaguely resembled a Macy's catalog. In retrospect, my parents may have felt this same sentiment while they were growing up as well. My father, the youngest of seven, grew up in the Midwest in the 70s and enlisted in the military at a young age to escape his tumultuous upbringing. My mother, also the baby of her family, is South Texan enamored with John Hughes films and 80s pop more than her own cultural roots. While Latino, in name, they both led lives that felt disconnected from their roots.

My childhood echoed that disconnection; I later learned that the phrase *ni de aquí, ni de allá* (neither from here nor there) clouded my youth and the lives of nearly all Latinos in the United States. This feeling first resonated with me while living in the predominantly white suburbia of the early 2000s; I felt a significant lack of representation in this community. This feeling of isolation only deepened when, in 2004, we moved to South Texas to be closer to my mother's family. The move plunged me into deep uncertainty despite my parent's noble attempt to support and stabilize my younger siblings. My opinions on the move were dismissed as irrelevant. After all, what could a 10-year-old contribute to such decisions? This invalidation of my feelings was a crushing blow, fueling an anger that became a central theme of my youth.

In Texas, I was the "whitewashed" newcomer in a place I was assured would feel more like home. I was finally not a novelty; things were supposed to be better because my last name could finally be pronounced correctly. However, that was not the case; middle school was a battleground where this anger manifested into negative self-thought and low self-esteem. I was awkward, quiet, and often misinterpreted as shy when I was just bracing for disappointment. Though I never stood a chance at being accepted, my outsider status was clocked immediately by my peers, who saw me as too different. I didn't need to convince myself I didn't fit in; they made it clear by calling me *Gringa* when I failed their cultural tests. This was no longer a manifestation of my insecurities; I was validated in my disdain for disappointing people, and my fierce irritability was justified. South Texas only became more alienating, and I felt more out of place among my Latino peers than I ever did around non-Latinos in California. The label "whitewashed" clung to me painfully, fueling my growing resentment that I began to project outward. I hid behind a facade of outward cynicism and what I thought were clever comebacks, earning me a less popular reputation amongst my classmates and family. By 13, I had embraced the contrarian role, challenging every norm, distancing myself from anything that hinted at mainstream or popular, as if my uniqueness would shield me from further rejection.

As I matured into adulthood, my bitter and self-conscious personality often revealed itself through unnecessarily aggressive and embarrassing interactions. It was not clear to me that my explosive outbursts were not so much about anger as they were about projecting my profound insecurities and fears onto those around me. I'd like to thank years of therapy for providing these insights, which is a treatment I sought out as an adult because growing up, we didn't struggle nearly enough to have those problems, or at least that was what was ingrained in us to believe.

Even today, in our Mexican-American household, the concept of mental health remains taboo. The legacies of our ancestral sacrifice and survival handed down from previous generations effectively stifled any open acknowledgment of personal mental struggles. How was I to question the adequacy of our life when all my basic needs were met? This looming history made it difficult to acknowledge or discuss personal mental struggles openly.

I understand that it is crucial to extend grace to adults raised in immigrant families who navigate mental health with limited knowledge and resources. I also understand that they often did the best they could with the information available to them. However, I will die on the hill that enforces the importance of holding said adults accountable for the need to evolve beyond these constraints.

Corajuda, initially a jokey nickname used to describe my temperament, unfortunately, became a dismissive badge for complex behaviors that were neither explored nor understood, fixed into my identity as something unchangeable rather than a trait that could be managed and healed. I'm nowhere near close to being seen as a healed human being. Still, I can recognize and empathize with both the imperfections and the efforts of our elders in addressing mental health, which can help hold space for a more understanding path for future generations.

I am aware that my experiences, while deeply personal, are far from unique. Growing up as a young person of color in the United States is filled with challenges that many face; navigating identity, confronting stereotypes, and feeling *ni de aquí, ni de allá*. My experiences, once sources of pain and confusion, have become the fuel and match that lit a passionate fire of activism within me. I am grateful, yet I remain introspective for every moment that has pushed me to explore the depths of my strength and capability. These experiences molded me, teaching me to embrace my

Latino heritage and the aspects of my personality I once questioned—my boldness, courage, and spirit.

This year, I turn 30; I look forward to embracing who I have become and who I will continue to evolve into as I leave behind my 20s. I enter this new decade of my life with humility, and I eagerly await to be confronted with similar lessons of my past that will guide my steps forward. In reclaiming my identity and reshaping my story, I am not just surviving but thriving as a proud *corajuda* Latina. I don't believe I am the constantly angry person I once was. I've learned to channel my passion into constructive avenues, advocating for societal changes that affect marginalized communities.

Once used against me as an insult but now worn as a badge of honor, I proudly reclaim the nickname *corajuda*. It is a sign of my journey and a reminder of how far I have come.

Gabriela Claudia Ochoa recently relocated from San Diego, California, to St. Louis, Missouri. Her service journey was shaped by her experiences growing up. Disparities in access to essential basic needs motivated her pursuit of a career and education in healthcare.

Her commitment to service was further solidified when she joined the Navy, where she gained insight into the challenges faced by veterans and military personnel. These experiences led to her pursuing various roles in veterans' hospitals and as a congressional staffer, allowing her to advocate for military and veteran communities and navigate the complex and frustrating bureaucratic red tape that hinders access to services.

Now as a nonprofit program manager, she focuses on the North County region, a historically underserved region predominantly populated by people of color. As a new author, Gabriela is eager to find a community with people who resonate with her stories.

Contact information for Gabriela can be accessed here.

Tamara Landeiro

My Leap of Faith

Some claim that my journey was very easy. At my restaurant, I share my experiences with my Cuban customers, who come in with nostalgia. I can remember every moment. I had a few steps to go, but I don't know how my heart could be divided. My daughters' footprints seemed big to me when their feet were so tiny. The bridge was so long, and the Rio Grande looked like a monster from my nightmares. Seconds seemed like hours, and I tried to look sideways, but my eyes didn't see anything else. They just didn't work. My mind was focused on the officer I saw in the distance waiting to receive us. A mix of determination, fear, and hope took control of my body. As I walked, I thanked the forbidden coins of Washington that someone kept in Havana and gave to me to pay the bridge toll.

Besides the significant risk of kidnapping, extortion, and other threats, the journey was easier than most. Nevertheless, my story of resilience traces back to a period well before we arrived in the United States.

Only forced by a love greater than myself could I escape from Cuba and my doctrines. A feat I once thought impossible was winning my internal conflict of desiring to assert my own voice while grappling with a pang of guilt. There was a shadow cast by the beliefs endlessly forced onto me throughout my existence.

My eldest daughter, Thalia, was an 11-year-old girl who possessed a determination beyond her young age: becoming a Woman Chess Grandmaster, like those of the stories of the old magazines that I used to read her as part of the bedtime routine, night after night. She always carried her chessboard everywhere. She used to keep a pawn under the pillow every night. Chess captivated her before she even had any idea of what multiplication was. My task as a mother was to support a girl who worked hard and was incredibly confident in her journey.

After tournaments, classes, days on the sidewalks seeing her playing…I knew that I didn't have a penny more to pay for her tournaments. The same limited resources and scarcity that each Cuban faced to live, she also needed to overcome to grow as a chess player.

On the other hand, did I want to pass her my testimony of strength and enduring spirit over a precarious economy? Over the years, I have seen many young women struggling for survival, marrying older foreign men to have the opportunity to live a better life in another country. Something that, to this day, is impossible to judge. When you don't have a place to live and when you live in a country where there are no laws that protect young girls from being prostituted at a young age, there is nothing to say.

The patriotic sentiment and unifying ideology of not abandoning your family was already implanted in my hypothalamus at birth. I grew up without being able to give an opinion about it. Thinking was already punished. I was always afraid that they could read or even imagine my thoughts. I still believe that, on the island where I was born, they can infiltrate the lives of every single person.

By inheriting this fear of communism, I also inherited my grandmother's demons. She taught me the wonders of cooking but also not to have material ambitions. To be humble or, rather, not to dream of anything was the right thing to do, to resist any temptations and endure the struggles of our current world.

It was very clear that dreaming of a life without power outages and constant hunger was already treason. There was a betrayal of the revolutionary doctrine and of the family. I was told that everyone outside the bubble lived a materialistic and egocentric life, so there was no right to speak out. The desire to be truly free was already a sin.

As a little girl, I was raised to be quiet and look adorable in my little dresses. There isn't a day that goes by that I don't appreciate my mother's wonderful sewing skills. The words still ring in my head at the neighborhood meetings, where others questioned why I was wearing nice clothes that my mother had brought from her trip as a student abroad. It was 1985, and wearing Levi jeans in Havana was more than questioned. It was punished along with ambitions to own a car or buy more than one toy a year for your child. Those who left Cuba were seen as the lowest of scum. It had been normal to assault them and throw eggs at their homes. Their decision to turn away from communism was perceived as irredeemable.

The fact that I understood at a very early age to keep a point in the mouth (that was what it was called to remain silent) did not mean that every now and then I was the wrong voice out loud my ongoing doubts. It occurred to me to speak out, and I repeat, it *occurred* to me to speak out.

It's a shame that one day, the school principal complained to my mother because I had told the education agency that in our school, there was no drinking water or any water at all. I realized that I had unnecessarily and incorrectly spoken the truth, even though they had asked about how we felt in our school. I had expressed my true feelings. I learned that, even if I reported it, nothing was going to be solved. It was better to be quiet so as not to be scolded.

I always tried to be obedient and not think about wanting more than blackouts almost every night and to take the bus to school to arrive at 8 a.m. after having waited for it since 5 a.m. I was fortunate; at the age of 18, I had lived much better than others on the island. We never had to eat a cat so as not to die of hunger during the crisis like other neighbors. We had a roof. It was a humble one, but one the tropical cyclones in the Caribbean did not devastate.

I remember my father's reaction when I told him I was leaving the country back in 2014. The shock on his face quickly changed to a sign to lower my voice. My grandmother had already passed, but I don't know if I would have had the same courage to express my decision to her. My mother, who loves her granddaughters so much, did not judge me.

We did not tell anyone else. I was not looking for approval in other people's eyes. This had to be done in silence. In chess, you must remain calm and collected while executing your plans so as not to give any hints to the opponent of what's to come. That had to be us, but we were playing with our lives.

We had a visa to Mexico, which had been thankfully granted to us. Under sweat and tears, I had made the decision to get to St. Louis, Missouri. I had never heard of this city outside of a few mentions in geography class during my school years. All I cared about St. Louis was that they were home to the best chess club in the United States, which could help my eldest daughter improve. I found this information after a few minutes of bad internet in the first moments I discovered that I was Googling at 35 years old. Nothing outside the bubble of the island was known to us. That is why after deleting the search history, I also made false searches for communist political doctrines, in case they checked or looked.

When the time came, I left the island, and thanks to this daring decision, my daughter Thalia became a chess grandmaster a few years later and my youngest daughter Tania has achieved incredible feats in arts and academics. Most importantly, they will never have to be silent. Every day I remind them, with my actions and words, that it is important to think, express, demonstrate, and question everything around them. Understand their privileges but never settle. They will be proudly loud while expressing their dreams.

While driving my car to my Cuban restaurant, I think about my decisions as an entrepreneur and businesswoman. Sometimes I'm afraid of wanting to have ambitions to live better, but when that happens, I cook more. I learn more, I work harder, and I prepare myself to do better. Because the day I chose to fight for my dreams and give my family a better life, was the day I realized I could.

Doors of opportunities have opened to us thanks to my leap of faith. The little, quiet girl I was raised to be decided that her words counted, her dreams and aspirations were valid, and chose to fight for them every day. I still face my demonic doctrines daily, but I lock my demons in cages so as not to pass them on to my daughters. I am healing my wounds by talking, sharing my experiences, and standing up for my own beliefs. I am proud to raise my voice because it has made my silent soul a vibrant one.

Tamara Landeiro is the owner and chef of Havana's Cuisine, a restaurant in St. Louis dedicated to sharing with the community the delights of traditional Cuban food. With a background in accounting and finances from the University of Havana, she is also an entrepreneur and active member of the Hispanic Chamber of Commerce of Metro St. Louis.

In 2021, she celebrated the grand opening of the Havana's Cuisine restaurant. Havana's has been awarded "STL 100 Best St. Louis Restaurants" for the last three years. The Tampa Cuban Sandwich from Havana has been awarded Best 2023 St. Louis sandwich by the *Riverfront Times* magazine. It is also one of the Best 10 Sandwiches in St. Louis.

With success rising every year, Tamara Landeiro and her daughters, Thalia and Tania, are so proud of the success and honored to represent Cuba in such a positive light.

Contact information for Tamara can be accessed here.

Ana Sayers

Just Do It: My Journey of Faith

If I could share one piece of advice for success, it would be—just do it. Never quit. Don't let fear stop you from pursuing your dreams. Do it scared. Do it tired. Do it even when you feel like you have nothing left. God will provide all your needs.

My journey really started at the age of 18 when I came to the United States from El Salvador. My mom booked me a flight, handed me a small luggage filled with clothes and $200 cash, and sent me on a life-changing journey. No instructions were included. I didn't know where to go or what to do. Although I was born in Houston, Texas, I was raised in El Salvador. I was not prepared for the culture shock. My path was set to stay with a family that was not the best advisor or in the best environment to pursue my dreams.

I had so many fears. The first time I faced my fear was in my Algebra class while I was attending school. My accent was very big, and I spoke very little English. I was scared to even raise my hand to ask to go to the bathroom. This was the first time here that I raised my voice. Something was telling me to take a break and go to the bathroom. I didn't need to use the bathroom, but some voice was telling me to go. At this time, I had no money and no food. With no friends, I would sit alone in the cafeteria each day with nothing to eat and no one to talk to. I was always so hungry. Because I was so shy, I was too scared to ask for help. Deep in my heart, I knew I had a voice, but I didn't know how to speak up or advocate for myself. My only friend was Jesus. He was the one I spoke with every day. He took care of me. That day I asked to go to the bathroom. I felt God leading me, and in the bathroom, I found $20 on the floor. That was my first $20 from nothing. My faith was so great I went to church, and I gave $10 to the church and kept $10 for me. That was my first lesson in the law of reaping and sowing—*La lay de la siembra y la cosecha*. Every seed you sow in faith, you will receive in a harvest. That $10 lasted much longer than what seemed possible. It was the first time I knew I wasn't alone and that God was with me.

One day I came home to the family I was staying with. My luggage was at the front door, and I was told I couldn't live there anymore. I found myself homeless without knowing where to go. I had only been here six months. I didn't know what to do. I called every person I knew in Houston, and no one could help me.

I was finally able to reach someone I met at church. They were kind enough to give me a place to stay. My church family provided a home when I had nowhere to go. During that time, I had to quit school and I needed to get a job to be able to buy food. The church family provided work for me to work from 7 a.m. to 6 p.m. at night for $100 a week. I was cleaning their house, babysitting, and working in their food truck. While I was grateful for the work, my heart cried out for more. I always wanted more for myself. My vision was to be a businesswoman in an office, but I didn't know how to do it.

I got a job at a newspaper where I would take three buses to get to work. I didn't know that on a holiday there was no public transportation. It was snowing one day, and I had no coat. I sat in the snow, waiting for a bus that would never arrive. I was crying out to God. I told him I felt abandoned. I felt like he wasn't listening to my prayers, but I trusted Him. He is my God and would remember my name. I remember that specific prayer like it was today.

I finally made it to the office, and they fired me for being late. I don't even remember how I got home that day. I picked up the newspaper and started looking for a new job. I applied for every job on a specific street because I knew the bus routes and there were a lot of businesses. Fierce determination pushed me forward. I got a job selling English Encyclopedias that helped people learn English when I couldn't even speak English. Money started to come in, but I couldn't afford a car yet. The new job did help me finally get a cell phone and better clothes. Every day was filled with prayer. I would pray for safety every day because the neighborhoods were not safe, but I knew God was with me. My prayer and faith in God guided me through the process.

I worked there until I had to move to another area. I wanted to change my circumstances to succeed so I could help my family in El Salvador. I wanted to pursue a career and build a better life. A new family brought me in and treated me like a daughter. I moved to a different side of town, and my life took a new turn. I went to work at Marshalls. I grew during my time there and was promoted, but in my heart I wanted more. I got fired from that job for a minor mistake two months after I was praying for a new opportunity. Sometimes God answers our prayers in unexpected ways. There are times doors have to shut so new ones can be opened.

If you feel hurt, hopeless, or uncertain, give it to the Lord. If you feel like you have no future, just give it to God and watch him work. I was willing to do anything with integrity to pursue my dreams. Work clean. Be genuine and give the best you have and watch opportunities begin to develop.

A door opened for me to be a secretary at an insurance agency. This began a journey of me starting a career that would become my future. I had no idea what insurance even was or how important it was for everyone to have. With insurance, I bought my first car. I had no license and no credit. My friend sent me to buy a car, and I walked out of the dealership with a brand-new Nissan with low interest rates with no license. I didn't know how to drive. I remember sitting in the car feeling so great, but Houston highways are crazy. I remember my dad told me as a child that driving was no big deal. He said to drive it straight and use your turn signals. He made it very simple. That was what I remembered when I put the car in drive. I made it to the other side of the city in my new car on my way to the Department of Motor Vehicles. I got my license and took it back to the dealership to show them my new license and insurance. I felt a new sense of freedom with that process.

Insurance became my career. With this incredible career, I was able to bring my family from El Salvador. I was able to buy myself a new car and my first home. I became an agency manager. Then, my career progressed to a recent promotion to Vice President, working for one of the largest agencies in the world. My journey took me from being homeless with $0 to a place to stay with $20 to building a career in insurance as a Latina with a strong accent. My accent is not my limitation. It's my challenge. It is a challenge I face every day. I could have done none of this without God guiding every step and providing for every need.

I have no other explanation than God. My advice now is to lose your fears and pursue your dreams. If you feel there is something stopping you from your dreams, just do it anyway. Don't dwell on the things that happened to you or the pain of the past. You are going to fail. Don't think about the failures. They are part of the process that leads you to the next step. Have faith in God. Put your dreams in God's hands, and He will take care of you. I live my life by Psalm 23 and know that He is my Shepherd. He has already promised that He will guide you. He will be there for you. When you have him on your side you won't have a need for anything. He will be your provider. Never stop dreaming. The sky is not the limit—there is more.

Ana Sayers has served the insurance industry for 17 years. She joined the USI Insurance Services- St. Louis office in November 2021 as a Commercial Line Producer within the construction insurance division. She was recently promoted to Vice President-Property & Casualty Risk Consultant, licensed in Illinois and Missouri.

She began her career in 2007. After eight years of running an agency, she was hired by ACCC Insurance Company in 2014. In 2019 she was relocated to Glen Carbon, Illinois, by AAdvantage Insurance Group as a Commercial Line Producer.

Ana graduated from State Auto exclusive PaceSetter sales development program. Ana received her Commercial Lines Coverage Specialist (CLCS) designation from The National Underwriter Company.

Ana lives in Glen Carbon, Illinois, with her husband, Gunnery Sergeant Matthew Sayers, and her stepson, Noah. Her hobbies include outdoor activities, church, gym, listening to music and podcasts, reading books, and spending quality time with family and friends.

Laura Torres

How Did I Get Here?
Not So Calladita, for Sure!

I have always associated procrastinating with being cool or creative and delivering the best of my work. It also concerns personal traumas and life situations that always pushed my priorities toward the end of the line. I was conditioned early on to be this way by my role model, my mother. It's not her fault, but I observed most of my adult life how she put her needs, personal plans, and even her health toward the end of the checklist. Why? I don't know. Perhaps her mom did the same. These women in our culture always carried so much weight from everyone else, yet never prioritized their needs. The *Machismo* experience is accurate, and today, it continues to influence many of my decisions.

I am proud that my "type" of procrastination regarding personal priorities ends with me. The culture of not prioritizing oneself ends with me. Even though some bad habits are hard to let go of, I am proud to say that I have planted some general rules that I hope my daughters are following. They know they are the most critical self before anyone else. *Mujeres* before me were not given the freedom to walk away from the mental pressure of feeling selfish or cared for, tangled in caring for everyone else before themselves. Can we blame the *Machistas* in our life?

Perhaps. In full context, this type of pressure and expectations to be in between two different jobs has made me stronger and more determined to pursue my career goals, calla-dita, and work on myself always behind the scenes. I have finally arrived at my destination. Procrastination has followed me along the way.

I arrived late to the professional career giveaway. I have learned that we take detours to prepare for the grand opening and the mature life event so we can handle it how it needs to be. I am finally arriving and feel very accomplished. I was an aspiring Latina leader early in my career. My success was measured by how my mom measured her success. In her mind, success was making it to the front office. She motivated me often to go to school so I could land a better job than she did. She said, "Study *Mija*, so you are not working like a *burro* like me."

How Did I Get Here?

It all began with Hubby's transition from active duty to retirement from the military. As a young military couple, we needed money. A military salary was insufficient. Most enlisted families are always struggling or financially restricted. My *machista* husband never saw it this way. I spent many years of my young married life with one foot in the door and another ready to walk away. I always had to justify my career aspirations. Often, I was made to feel like a lousy wife and a neglectful mother for wanting to be part of the workforce. I cannot fully blame him for being how he was. His own family culture and role models in his personal life set up unrealistic expectations on what the ideal "wife" or home life needed to be to battle taboos. As he battled personal demons, trust issues, and cultural taboos, he challenged me.

Finding full-time work and securing a more prosperous career right before he was getting ready to leave the military was like finding a needle in a haystack. He often told me I could work once he retired. To work in harmony, I needed to secure a particular work style, a niche, and a work environment to get his approval. I searched for four years before landing the job that would give his *machismo* mindset peace of mind and my dream job. Through numerous conflicts, many spousal fights, and so many silent treatments, I trained *calladita* to make it to where I am. Navigating this road has been difficult once I started my professional journey.

I trained *calladita* to get to where I am. My determination was like no other. I was hooked once I began to taste what it felt like to be part of the workplace, to have a great demeanor, and to work professionally. I wanted to make my husband and myself happy. For many years, I wanted to feel his approval and be part of the workplace. Still, I always felt that was never enough. I now know that if you are going to do things in life, you have to do it for yourself. Leave all external opinions out of your way. He now knows that work has been good for us, but it felt at moments like he was my biggest roadblock.

Since I began my professional journey, I have always been a hard worker. Despite not being allowed or receiving full approval, I collected over 15 years of combined experience in many areas, *calladita*, with approval and others without authorization. I built a solid career based on dedication, excellence, and many undefined moments. Despite my professional accomplishments, I experienced difficult situations at work and home. Just when I thought I had finally made it, for the first time in my professional life, I began to face bullying in the workplace and micro-aggressions, and I didn't understand why. A new woman in the office had just started to work with me, but soon, she began to feel threatened by my optimistic and cheerful can-do attitude. I was so excited I had found the perfect job, which fulfilled me and allowed me to do purposeful work. I also met my husband's requirements for me to be focused on work. While a co-worker was so mean at work, I was experiencing constant arguments at home. Even though my husband was moving toward retirement, I was still responsible for caring for everything at home.

It was a dark period in my professional life. These experiences at work made me feel isolated and unsure of how to address the issue without jeopardizing my job. I needed to keep this job and not walk away because it was one of those situations that fulfilled my husband's guidelines for me to be included in the workplace. Meanwhile, the husband's *machismo* attitude at home made me feel even more trapped. He dismissed my career achievements, belittled my opinions, and insisted I prioritize homemaking over my professional ambitions.

Despite these challenges, I was not ready to give up. I deserved better and decided to take control of my career journey. I started by reaching out to a few trusted colleagues and sharing my workplace bullying experiences. Surprisingly, their support was a turning point in my journey. It showed me the power of solidarity in the face of adversity. The sense of community and support in the workplace was crucial to my professional journey.

The work environment leveled up, harmony took over, and great bosses joined with inspiring leadership. With struggles still at home, I sought support from a women's empowerment group, started attending leadership conferences, and volunteering. I gained new perspectives and strategies to communicate more effectively, but most importantly, I decided to prioritize myself. I began communicating better with my husband and gained his support. Tragic events in our family life took priority. He finally realized that life can be so fragile. While this was all happening, I learned to set boundaries and expressed my needs calmly yet firmly; I adopted the Mexican term, *Me vale madre*.

Patience and a few health setbacks have transformed his temperament and calmed him. I would like to report that it was all because he became this supportive husband, and maybe he did, but he never forgets to remind me of how he has allowed me to work. I am content to say that ever since I decided to *Me vale madre*, because regardless of what I did, he was still not happy. I *calladita* chose to focus on my career, grow my area of expertise, and maybe break his rules from time to time. I have flourished with newfound confidence, and with my mom by my side and my kids, I have created a more supportive environment that shows my daughters that they don't need the approval of anyone. I have now realized that by standing up for myself and seeking support from my mentors, I improved my life and inspired my kids to do the same.

My journey is not unique, yet not easy. It has been an experience of empowering moments. I faced many challenges head-on, particularly in the environments where they were supposed to be the safest. Fortunately, I have come out stronger on the other side. I know my worth and am determined to live a life that reflects it. I am finding my voice and keep spreading it to others who, like me, experience systems that attempt to hold them back. My journey is proof of the empowerment that comes from overcoming challenges and righting the *machismo* and ridiculous guidelines that set Latinas 10 miles behind everyone else.

I feel so strong and can call myself a beacon of strength and a *chingona*. When I see my journey, I can see that one can overcome any obstacle and rewrite one's story with courage and resilience.

Laura Torres is the Associate Director of Workforce Engagement and Diverse Talent Sourcing for a recognized nonprofit. She supports military spouse career initiatives and program outreach. Laura facilitates the training and development of career ambassadors and ensures the careers program mission reaches its full potential.

She obtained her Bachelor of Arts in Liberal Studies with a concentration in Early Childhood Education from EOU and an MBA with a concentration in Human Resource Management from National University. She holds multiple marketing and information technology certifications.

After relocating to California and being unable to find satisfying work, Laura had to re-train in a new career to advance in a competitive community. She volunteers for SVOs and supports local civilian organizations.

As a military caregiver, she enjoys life with her retired veteran husband, who served in the Marine Corps for 21 years. They have four beautiful grown children and enjoy Pacific Northwest life.

Contact information for Laura can be accessed here.

Tais Kraljevic

Into and Out of the Danger Zone: Always Trust Your Gut and Your People

Through World War II and the Korean War, dogfighting was the prevalent form of air battles and raids. If you have seen any movies or TV shows set during these conflicts, you will recognize the close-range shootouts where skilled pilots steered their aircraft in whirlwind maneuvers as the crew aimed their machine guns to shoot down the enemy. In the 1950s, new technologies such as advanced RADARs and guided missiles enabled pilots to deploy weapons at long range. This changed how military fighter aircraft were designed and led the Air Force to change its focus to developing a new air-superiority fighter. In the late 1960s, the "F-X" program was announced. Its aim was to design and build an aircraft that had a high thrust-to-weight ratio (acceleration), high speed, a high-visibility cockpit, and both long- and close-range target potential (high maneuverability and capable of carrying heavy weapons for long distances).

In 1969, aerospace manufacturer McDonnell Douglas, located in St. Louis, Missouri, was awarded the contract and went on to develop the F-15 Eagle fighter jet. Three years later, on July 27, 1972, test pilot Irv Burrows made history when he flew the first F-15 for the first time. The first combat F-15 was delivered to the U.S. Air Force fleet two years later, and it exceeded all expectations.

Fast forward to the summer of 2022. It has been 50 years since Irv Burrows made history, and the Boeing Defense, Space, and Security St. Louis site was getting ready to celebrate. The F-15 program office would host a ceremony to commemorate this momentous milestone with current Boeing employees working the F-15 program, U.S. Air Force leadership, and special guests such as Irv Burrows himself and the McDonnell family. One of the many things that made this ceremony so special is that usually ceremonies are held to inaugurate new aircraft. The brand-new F-15EX Eagle II, a direct descendant of the original F-15 Eagle, had its maiden flight and inauguration ceremony in early 2021. A year later, we were celebrating 50 years of flight. It was a full-circle moment and a reason to be proud for all St. Louis employees.

I know it sounds corny to talk about a ceremony this way, and I admit that I am sentimental and a little *melosa*, but I was heavily invested since I was part of the planning team for the ceremony. I had just taken a new role to be the executive assistant to the Vice President Program Manager of the F-15 program. This person's job was to ensure we kept modernizing and selling F-15s.

The day of the ceremony, I realized that this event also highlighted something important in my personal life. Sitting there, waiting for my cue to bring a gift to the stage, I realized I had achieved my childhood dream.

As a teenager, I dreamt about being a fighter jet pilot (specifically F/A-18s, Navy-flown, and Boeing-built). I was introduced to the world of military aircraft through *Top Gun*, the movie about the Naval Fighter Weapons School with Tom Cruise. Up until that point, I had wanted to be a commercial pilot, but as Kenny Loggins sang the last verse of "Danger Zone," I realized that fighter jets were my true calling. As time went on,

I figured things out about myself and my priorities that made me realize a life in the military was not the right fit for me. Engineering and a civilian life interested me more than enlisting in or applying to the Naval Academy, but my passion for these aircraft never went away. The specifics of the dream looked a little bit different than it did 15 years ago. I shot for the moon and landed among the stars.

This does not mean that the desire to be a pilot is gone. It will never be gone. I will always wonder what it's like to feel the adrenaline rush of take-off and after completing a mission. Pilots get to live in glory, like heroes in movies, but it all comes with so much risk and many sacrifices—sacrifices I was not willing to make. What about the sacrifices I have made and am willing to make or the risks I have taken? Danger zones do not exist only in war. We, as humans simply living life, enter places and situations with no known risk of harm, failure, and other negative consequences. These danger zones are trickier since there are no intelligence briefings or months to years of training. We leap into them bravely. At the core of every mission, success comes from the decisions made in a split second and the team's ability to work together. I believe that these two are the only things we need to get through any danger zone: our instincts that help us make the best decisions and our support networks.

The first danger zone I encountered in my life was one fought by my parents. In 2006, my father was granted a three-year H-1B work visa to immigrate to the United States with his immediate family. Facing economic uncertainty and political unrest, my parents chose to take the opportunity and never looked back. They left behind family, lifetime friendships, degrees, a language they spoke with ease and grace, knowledge of entire infrastructures and systems, great food, work-life balance, a sense of community, delicious food, and their savings. An entire bank account in Bolivia is no match to the expenses in the United States. In

2009, my parents bought the home they continue to live in after spending years believing they would never be able to.

The next danger zone fell on me as I navigated the schooling and educational system, then further into the workplace. Like my parents had to figure out entire systems on their own, I had to understand the process to prepare for college, apply to college, apply to FAFSA (Free Application of Federal Student Aid), and choose a good career. Through research and a lot of conversations with counselors and teachers, I chose Florida Atlantic University to get my Mechanical Engineering degree.

My sophomore year of college, I was encouraged by a good friend to attend the Society of Hispanic Professional Engineers (SHPE) national career fair. I was convinced I had no chance of finding a job there, but we banded together with the Florida International University SHPE chapter to prepare. I attended my first SHPE conference, loaded with information from students who had attended previously and coaching from professional engineers who volunteered after work hours. To my very shock, I came out with two co-op offers. My people helped me get there.

When I accepted both job offers, I had to take a total of three semesters off school to work full-time. Many people suggested against it, afraid this would damper my education somehow. I knew these were incredible opportunities that would help me get a head start in building my career. Later, I was able to get part-time engineering jobs close to campus, and by the time I graduated, I had six full-time job offers. My gut feeling had paid off.

I started working for Boeing in 2019 in the F/A-18 manufacturing line (building my dream fighter jets!). Unfortunately, there were many complications in my first role. The team faced several ethics complaints, and I felt unfulfilled by the work. I was advised against switching teams or jobs since I was a new hire and did not want to be perceived as a "puddle-jumper." I then proceeded to switch roles three times in two years. I went from production engineering to flight test, into electrical engineering. With a mechanical degree, I was a bit delusional taking on that role, but I am glad I did. I loved the job and thrived in it. Two years later, people in my network who knew of my goal to become a program manager encouraged me to apply for the executive assistant role. This was another wild leap. The EA role propelled my career forward, and I am now a manager in the Sensors group, where we develop RADARs and electro-optical sensors for the F-15, F/A-18, and other platforms. It could not be a better fit.

I am very fortunate I get to say that I have my dream job. I can say my hard work and killer instinct got me here, but it would not be true. Without the people in my life, I would not have been able to achieve any of it. The formula for building a strong support network is to connect with people continuously and openly. This can be intimidating, but trust that your gut will lead you to the right people. Push through the doubts and seek people out.

Wherever you are in life, whatever danger zone you find yourself in, do not hesitate to lean on your people. Your team will always get you out and back home safely.

Tais was born in Cochabamba, Bolivia, and migrated to the United States with her family at the age of 12. She grew up in South Florida and attended Florida Atlantic University in Boca Raton, Florida. She graduated with her bachelor's degree in mechanical engineering in 2018.

Tais started out in the automotive industry before taking a role with Boeing in St. Louis, Missouri, in 2019, where today she is an electrical engineering manager. Her passion is mentorship, as she attributes her successes to the mentorship she has received and her involvement in organizations like the Society of Hispanic Professional Engineers (SHPE). Most recently, she joined the SHPEtinas track of the SHPE St. Louis chapter, which focuses on supporting Latinas and Women of Color in STEM. Tais hopes to inspire people to chase their wildest dreams, as scary and intimidating as they may be. This anthology is her debut as a writer.

Edda Berti

Crossroads:
My Own Path and Foreign Side Roads
of Life Experiences to Freedom

I am part of a vast Hispanic population who immigrated to the United States. It's estimated that there are 65 million Hispanic people living in America. Most of us came here seeking freedom, autonomy, and dreaming of the possibility to follow our passions. I had a long journey to achieve these dreams that have taken unexpected twists and turns.

In the 1980s, I lived in Peru. The political and economic landscape was shadowed by the rise of the terrorist groups *Shining Path* and *MRTA*. We lived under constant confrontations between the terrorists and the military. Our lives took a path of fear and confusion, terrorized by explosions, assassinations, blackouts, interrupted roads, vehicles set on fire, and curfews.

Even through these awful events, we carried on with our lives. I was a student at the university. I founded a nonprofit called Humanitarian Association of Huaral. My group, formed by university students and friends, decided to help the health district of the town where my parents resided. Our partners were providing the training for 120 technical nurses in a year. They could administer first aid, antibiotics, shots, and vaccines and have knowledge in nutrition after completing the training. It was a deeply felt need since the rural areas had few medical services. The mayor of the city helped cover part of the cost to pay for the students but not for the teachers. We organized a public collection named "Colecton." We raised more than double what was needed.

We were preparing for the graduation celebration. The mayor told us the Minister of Health and his executive team were coming to attend the graduation. They would search for everyone to provide security for the officials coming. He asked me if I knew this, and I said, "No." So, the mayor said, "Before the event, I will make him an illustrious member of the city, and then he will be yours." The ceremony, the food, and the folkloric presentations were unforgettable. A year later, I married the minister. Since then, the mayor always said jokingly, "I did not know that you would take my words so seriously."

My freedom was even more limited due to the position my husband held. I would go with him to different parts of Peru, but we had to live in constant alert, changing routes to go to places, canceling events for security, and always heavily guarded. I almost lost my life a couple of times. While coordinating between the Ministries of Health and Fishing, I was supposed to inaugurate an industrial fridge there to hold frozen fish for three to six months to battle poverty and malnutrition in the area. It was a four-hour trip. We had stopped at the town of *Aramachay*, but we got lost. We arrived an hour late to discover a group yelling at us to turn back immediately because the community center we were going to was attacked by terrorists.

The second time, my husband and I went to the southern part of Peru, Arequipa, to celebrate 446 years of inception. The Federal Republic of Germany had donated equipment to implement a new laboratory in the local university. I was a month pregnant, and I did not feel well. I decided to stay at the hotel. We were on the third floor above the restaurant on the second floor.

When he and a local politician went to give the equipment, I remained looking at the beautiful plaza through the huge arched windows, looking at the people walking in the streets excited for the celebrations. I decided to take a shower, and I closed the curtains. I could not find my purse, so I opened the curtains again, and to my surprise, there was a shoe box sitting outside of the window. I called security immediately; the red berets and police and explosives department came rushing into my room. They found a plastic explosive wrapped in a woman's pantyhose. They discovered that the explosives were placed there by a 10-year-old boy who sold candies in the streets.

My 24-year-old brother Willy, a young lieutenant, was deployed to the emergency zone in *Tingo Maria* in the jungle. He would tell me that many of his troop members were brothers or relatives of the terrorists in the area. On Nov 7, 1990, he went with his unit to make a routine visit to the nearby town. They were ambushed. That day my brother and many of his soldiers lost their lives. Many of our Peruvian families lost someone in this war. A final report states that from 1980-2000, 69,280 people died or disappeared because of the armed conflict in my country.

Shortly after this, my husband accepted a job as representative of the Pan American Health Organization in Brazil. This change helped me cope with my loss and the challenging time of living in a country that does not resemble the land where I was born and raised.

I was so happy to arrive in a new country, ready to start working. Because of my visa status, I couldn't work, I could only study. I dedicated myself to studying, raising my two children, and participating in the way of life this position had to offer us. *Brasilia*, the capital of Brazil, is an incredibly unique city. All the administrative buildings looked futuristic and vast. I enjoyed the weekly gatherings in the embassies, learning about other cultures, their cuisine, their independence celebrations, their festivals, and tertulia. I have treasured long-lasting friendships since then. I will always be grateful for all the warm people of Brazil, where I experienced optimism and practicality.

After five years, I had to leave this incredible country and my marriage. I decided to come to the United States because I saw an opportunity for me to gain real freedom, to gain autonomy, and find my true self. It was a high price, but I do believe this country made me strong, independent, and helped me to redefine the way that I see life.

I arrived at my cousin's home in Hartsburg near Jefferson City, Missouri. I started learning English at Mizzou. My children enrolled in the schools. I thought my children could continue to have karate, ballet, and piano, but the reality is that there are so many hours in a day, and everything was on me. All the routines that I knew were not assisted by family or maids anymore. Groceries, meal preparation, cleaning, washing clothes, studying, helping the children with homework while doing my own homework, and repeat.

Months went by, and I couldn't feel the same enthusiasm that I had when I came. Some days, I would stop in the street before picking up my children from school and tears started to come down. I cried from exhaustion, longing for family, friends, tastes, smells, my cities' corners, the different way of life.

I felt strong and confident with the new language. I could communicate with the world! I decided immediately to move out of my cousin's home and have my first apartment. I could only furnish it with secondhand furniture. I reupholstered two sofas. I painted another one that ended up looking like an antique piece, sewed my own curtains, and repainted a table for the dining room. Nobody could tell that they were not brand new. I made our dinner table from logs and a top glass from Pier One. I carried the mattresses on the top of my car and looked for plants to make my space reflect me.

I enrolled in the graduate program of journalism. There were still bills to pay, including tuition and books, rent, utilities, phone, insurance, food, car, clothing, and more. Since I held a type of visa where one must be enrolled only as a full-time student, I started working under the table from 7 p.m. to 7 a.m. three times a week in an assisted living center. I worked for people with disabilities and mental health issues. I was trained to dispense their medication twice a day, prepare meals, serve their food, wash dishes, dispense their personal hygiene products and cigarettes, and give them a bath. Finally, while they were asleep, I washed and folded their clothing. Some weekends I drove the company van and took the residents to the mall for ice cream. It was hard work, but the sense of autonomy out of every space gained in this soil made me feel empowered.

After graduation, I reconnected with the consul of Peru in St. Louis—Rosa, and her husband, Luis. They were instrumental in settling my family in St. Louis. I started to work as a Director of Interpreting and Instruction. I held this job on and off for many years until 2018. I did my job diligently, but my mother would recall the times when I worked in the community back home. My eyes had this spark that was not there anymore. That same year my mother passed away. It took me three years to find balance and a job that could make my eyes have the spark again. I found this place in "Puentes de Esperanza," focusing on the long-term prosperity and stability of the immigrants in our community. We foster a sense of belonging and trust, encouraging them to actively participate and contribute to our community. We have a Welcome Center in Fairmont City, the third largest Latino population in Illinois, and are opening one in Chester, Illinois.

The United States helped me find independence. It gave me the opportunity to close the cycle by serving a community I hold dear through social programs and human development.

Edda Berti attained two bachelors of Art degrees: in business administration at the San Martin de Porres University of Lima, Peru, and Social Sciences-Sociology at the University of Brasilia, Brazil. Graduate studies in journalism were at the University of Missouri. She started her career as president of the organization "Humanitarian Association Huaral" in Peru and as a UNICEF consultant. Edda has served on the Goodwill Mers board since 2020. She enjoys spending time with her children and grandson. A great cook, her favorite dishes are *papa a la huancaina* and *picarones*! During the pandemic, she learned to prepare sourdough and cultivate potatoes, onions, strawberries, squash, tomatoes, and aromatic plants. Edda is fluent in five languages, enjoys poetry, is learning to play the piano, and is preparing to return to the university for leadership and social change. Her greatest passion is to be close and supportive to the families of the Hispanic community.

Leslie Hernandez

Breaking Tradition and Challenging the Notion of Retiring

In many Latin cultures, family is at the center of everything. There's a strong sense of duty to one's loved ones, and often, this extends into personal and professional life decisions. For many, the idea of retirement is filled with the expectation of caring for aging parents or other family members. The weight of these cultural norms can feel immense, especially for women who are often expected to take on the bulk of caregiving responsibilities. Challenging this belief system is necessary to create space for personal growth, professional fulfillment, and changing perceptions of what it means to honor family.

I founded *De Mi Madre Aprendí*, a Latina woman-owned small business. It is not just a tribute to my mother and cultural roots, but it is a way to break *free* from the restrictive belief that retirement is solely for taking on family responsibilities. It is an opportunity to enjoy a passion and fulfill a mission to help the community in need during the pandemic. Instead, we are redefining what it means to balance personal dreams, family, and the legacy we want to leave behind.

The Weight of Cultural Expectations

The idea that family comes first is a central tenet in Latin households. This often means that career aspirations are put on hold, or even abandoned, to focus on raising children or caring for elderly relatives. In my case, I passed that stage. I am in a stage where I will retire in the year 2024 after 38 years of working with children with different abilities and their families.

While these roles are crucial and worthy of respect, there's an inherent problem when we think this is the only way to do things. There is no option to demonstrate *liberation*. We are expected to follow what was taught as the only options presented to us.

This belief often goes unquestioned, passed down from generation to generation, but it's time to challenge it. We are living in a different century, and we are responsible, no matter our age, to make changes for justice and equity. My expectations consist of helping our community to accept one another with respect and an open heart.

Honoring Family, While Redefining Tradition

In 2020, during the pandemic, when we were confined to our homes, the families I supported were struggling to meet basic needs and support their children with distance learning.

The creation of *De Mi Madre Aprendí* was rooted in the desire to honor my mother, specifically the traditions and recipes passed down from my mother. However, it was also a way to carve out my own space in the world of business, food, and entrepreneurship. It was my opportunity to take the lessons I learned from my mother and use them as a foundation for something that was distinctly mine.

Through this venture, I was able to change the perception of what it means to honor my mother. Instead of viewing retirement as a full-time commitment to caregiving, I am redefining it as a phase of life that allows for both honoring my mother and pursuing a second personal passion. The two are not mutually exclusive.

Starting a business is no easy feat, especially when you are bucking cultural norms. It required me to break through not only my own internalized beliefs but also the expectations of those around me. Yet, I found strength in knowing that by stepping into this entrepreneurial space, I was creating a new path not only for myself but for the next generation.

A New Perception of Retirement

For many, the idea of retirement is synonymous with relaxation, leisure, and perhaps the occasional travel adventure. However, for women in Latin families, retirement often looks very different. It can signify the beginning of a new full-time job, one that revolves around caring for grandchildren, aging parents, or extended family members.

This perception of retirement is so ingrained that many women don't even question it. They anticipate it, prepare for it, and accept it as a natural part of life. This perception is beginning to shift, especially as more and more women are taking control of their financial futures and career trajectories.

For me, retirement doesn't mean stepping away from work to focus solely on family responsibilities. My two treasures, my children Patrilie and Jesus Mariano Rafael are grown adults that I am super proud of. My husband Rafael also helps with the food business when he can. That gives me the freedom to choose how I spend my time and energy, whether that's on my business, my family, or myself. This new perception of retirement is one that I hope to pass on to my children and to others in my community.

The Challenges of Breaking Tradition

Challenging deeply ingrained cultural beliefs is not without its struggles. There are moments of guilt, self-doubt, and even resistance from those closest to you. Stepping away from the traditional role of caretaker can feel like you're turning your back on your family, even when that's far from the truth.

There's also the external pressure to conform to members of the family or friends' expectations. People may question your decision to continue working or pursuing your passions when your family could use your help. They may not understand why you would choose entrepreneurship over the more "respectable" role of full-time caregiver or question if you are really doing it because you need the money.

However, these challenges are worth overcoming. By challenging these norms, we're not only creating a better life for ourselves but also for future generations. We're showing our children that it's okay to have ambitions outside of family care and that it's possible to strike a balance between personal fulfillment and familial responsibility.

Changing the Perception of My Era

When I established *De Mi Madre Aprendí*, I did so not only as a tribute to my mother but also as a way to change the perception of what women in my era are capable of. For too long, the expectations placed on women have been limiting and restrictive. By stepping into the world of business, I am proving that we can do more than what tradition dictates. This era is one of transformation. We are breaking *free* from the belief that women should retire to care for family and instead embracing the idea that retirement can be a time of exploration, innovation, and contribution. It's about rewriting the narrative and making room for new possibilities.

I hope that my story, and the story of *De Mi Madre Aprendí*, inspires others to challenge the norms in their own lives. Whether that's starting a business, pursuing a new passion, or simply choosing a different path, the key is to recognize that there is no one "right" way to honor your family, in my case, my mother, *Mama Pacha*. You can care for your loved ones while still pursuing your dreams. In fact, I believe that by following our passions, we're able to better serve our families in the long run.

The Legacy of Redefining Roles

As women continue to challenge these outdated perceptions, we are paving the way for future generations to have more freedom and flexibility in their lives. We are showing our daughters, nieces, and granddaughters that they can prioritize their dreams without sacrificing their familial roles. The legacy we leave is one of empowerment, choice, and balance. We are not alone.

The establishment of *De Mi Madre Aprendí* is part of that legacy. It is proof that women in my generation are not limited by the traditions of the past. We are creating new traditions, ones that honor our heritage while embracing our own desires for personal and professional growth.

By challenging the belief that retirement is solely for family responsibilities, we are opening up new opportunities for ourselves and for those who come after us. We are showing that it's possible to honor our families by living authentically and pursuing our passions. This is the legacy I want to leave. I leave a legacy that women are *free* to choose their own paths, balance their responsibilities in ways that make sense for them, and redefine what it means to honor family in the modern era.

The traditional notion of retirement as a time to take on family responsibilities is being challenged by a new generation of women who are determined to carve out space for their own dreams. Through ventures like *De Mi Madre Aprendí*, we are showing that it's possible to honor our families and our cultural roots while also pursuing personal and professional fulfillment. By changing the perception of what retirement can be, we are redefining roles, challenging outdated beliefs, and creating a legacy of empowerment for future generations. The belief that women should retire to care for family is no longer the only option. Instead, we are forging new paths that allow us to balance our love for family with our desire for personal growth and success.

Leslie Hernandez is the innovative force behind *De Mi Madre Aprendi*—from my mother, I learned—a vibrant line of Latin-flavor seasonings. As an entrepreneur, Leslie's journey began with a deep-rooted passion for traditional Puerto Rican cuisine, learned firsthand from her mother in Puerto Rico.

Her mother is renowned for her delectable Puerto Rican "Pasteles" and other simple, natural dishes. Her mother introduced Leslie to the values of love, humility, and community. Her mother's remarkable ability to feed her 16 children and extended family with limited resources inspired Leslie to create products that bring people together through food.

Today, Leslie channels this legacy into her brand, crafting high-quality marinades and seasonings that burst with rich flavors without relying on salt or artificial additives. With *De Mi Madre Aprendí*, Leslie aims to share the warm, familiar atmosphere of her mother's kitchen, delivering traditional Puerto Rican home cooking everywhere.

Contact information for Leslie can be accessed here.

Jacqueline Duty

Finding Freedom

Now the Lord is the Spirit: and where the
Spirit of the Lord is, there is liberty.
~2 Corinthians 3:17

To have a better understanding of a person's worldview, it is important to invest time into understanding their history. I have been so privileged to spend time with so many incredible women who have overcome adversity. They have learned the power of letting go of the pain of the past and moving forward into a hopeful future filled with potential.

The process of helping women write their stories has been life-changing for me. To be able to read their stories and more fully understand their tenacity and strength has created the motivation to take steps of letting go of things that have held me back.

My grandmother was a strong, independent woman who had the courage to flee the persecution of an evil dictator. She left Santiago, Chile, in the 1970s to pursue the freedom that was offered in the United States. She was able to return to rescue her four youngest children, but my mother and her sister were left behind due to their age and lack of ability to get a visa. They invested the next three years desperately working to get a visa to come to this country to see their family. My mother met my father and decided to let go of her life in Chile and build a new reality.

I can remember the day my mother received her citizenship. She invested time to learn the Constitution and the history of this country. She stood proudly with her hand over her heart and had tears running down her cheeks as she declared the Pledge of Allegiance for the first time as a United States citizen.

I grew up watching the strength of my parents as they fought to give my brothers and me a life they always dreamed of. It was never easy, but I witnessed their love for each other overcome the adversity and pain that life could deliver. I grew up not being allowed to speak Spanish because my father did not want us to feel the pain of prejudice that my mother experienced due to her heavy accent and lack of strong English vocabulary. It didn't bother me to not be allowed to speak Spanish because, for most of my childhood, I didn't speak much at all. I was always very shy and avoided talking to anyone. My family jokes that once I started talking, they couldn't get me to shut up.

I always felt deep down that my voice couldn't be heard. For years throughout childhood, teenage years, and even as an adult, I was constantly silenced. I would be interrupted in business meetings or even told to stop talking. I felt it was necessary to make my voice heard, so I found myself yelling in fights with family members or interrupting people at work because they would always interrupt me. It took time to heal from that and begin to understand the power of my voice. Once I gained an understanding of who I was and the value I could bring to a conversation, I no longer felt the need to have to speak. Today, I find myself talking less and listening much more. I can learn so much from every person I meet. I have learned to speak when I know I can bring value to the conversation.

Other than that, I sit back and watch and listen. We are in the information age with so much knowledge at our fingertips. There is so much to learn.

I have found the greatest revelations come when I can stop working so hard all the time and just take time to rest. In those moments, when I get quiet, I get clarity, peace, and revelation. This creates space for me to develop the thoughts that will bring forth the most wisdom, so when I speak, I know it will contribute to the conversation of the group I'm with.

I can sit in the board room and still get interrupted. I have a much better understanding today of why people feel the need to be the loudest or talk the most in the room. I've learned to leave the table when respect isn't being delivered because you can find a group that will value you, and your voice will be heard.

Today I am helping launch new artists as the co-owner of the Grafton Art Gallery. This gallery is designed to help artists tell their story through their art. It was built to engage people at the intersection of culture, patriotism, and community.

I also serve as Commissioner of Communications for the National Memorial of Military Ascent. The memorial will pay honor to the courage and sacrifice of all veterans. Inspired by the Army Rangers of Pointe du Hoc, the memorial will feature immersive exhibits and serve as a vital educational resource, honoring the legacy of our military. Visitors will be able to experience life-size bronze statues climbing the bluffs as they did on this pivotal day in history. An interactive museum will allow them to experience what it felt like to be in battle in various wars in our history.

It is so important for everyone to understand our history and honor the sacrifices made by those who fought for our freedom. Freedom isn't free. There is always a price. Without a cost, there is no value. Without understanding the sacrifice made, many people miss the value we have in the opportunity provided by our beautiful country. Unless you are Native

American, at some point, you or your relatives were immigrants. We need to lock arms in unity as people who are pursuing our purpose in a country that affords the most opportunity. Treasure it and honor those who serve our country every day.

A few years ago, I heard my mother speak to a group of high school kids about her journey to this country. She said, "I came to this country, and I found freedom, love, and Jesus. That is all I ever needed." I'm so thankful for the journey that brought me to the place I am now. I am in a country that affords the freedom to pursue purpose and find my voice. My voice is finally being heard. I just had to find the right group that honors people and does not tear them down. I highly encourage everyone to invest time in reading every person's story in this powerful book. Every woman here is a testimony to the tenacity, courage, and fire that flows through the blood of a Latina woman. These women are amazing and have a voice that will be heard around the world.

As I was sitting there enjoying my new views from a place of peace, I was inspired to write again. I found myself writing poetry after decades of avoiding it. It seems fitting to share the poem I wrote as I observed eagles soar above the lighthouse in beautiful Grafton, Illinois.

The Eagle's Rest
The eagle is mighty and strong, but not loud.
With wings that span, she soars high above the clouds.
Even eagles have frustrations in life that try to tear it down.
The crow will land on the eagle's back and bite her neck.
With consistent attacks the crow will peck and peck.

Through the attack, the eagle is not the same.
But she refuses to play the game.
No time or energy is spent on a rallying cry.

With no response, the mighty eagle soars high.
The higher she flies; the crow can't sustain.
The eagle will demonstrate how she reigns.
The crow will no longer be able to attack,
And then he will fall back.

The eagle continues to soar.
Gaining new sight and vision, she can now find the shore.
With a new vision through this experience, the eagle can land.
She will find a new place to stand.
Her courage and strength have proven she is the best.
Now she can take some time and just learn to rest.
-Jacqueline Duty

Jacqueline Duty is a Chilean artist, author, speaker, and marketing consultant. She invested a 20-year career in corporate media, working for metropolitan newspapers, magazines, 11 radio stations, and television for 20 years. She launched her own digital marketing agency and online media company in her pursuit to help businesses tell their story.

She is the Commissioner of Communication for the National Memorial of Military Ascent. As a part owner of the Grafton Art Gallery, she works with groups across the region to leverage art to help tell stories and launch artists into new levels of excellence.

She serves on the school board for Mississippi Valley Christian School and the Hispanic Chamber of Metro St. Louis. She also works closely with many civic organizations and enjoys spending her time with her husband and two sons, Tyler and Trevor.

Jacqueline remains dedicated to helping people pursue their purpose and achieve success.

Contact information for Jacqueline can be accessed here.

To the authors of *Calladitas Rising*:

Your stories matter. Your perspectives enrich our understanding. Your courage inspires change.

We believe in the power of diverse narratives to shape a more inclusive world. By sharing your experiences, you're not just contributing to literature—you're paving the way for future generations.

So, from all of us at Acumaxum – thank you. Keep writing, keep sharing, and keep inspiring. We're honored to be on this journey with you.

All the best,

Acumaxum

GRACIAS

We are honored to stand beside you on this journey, and we are so proud of the voices that are rising together in this book. Your stories will inspire and empower others, leaving an impact that will be felt for generations to come.

L A T I N A S   R I S I N G